guide

ROME
and the VATICAN

ats
italia
editrice

Piazza dei Cinquecento - Museo Nazionale Romano - Palazzo Massimo - Piazza della Repubblica - Baths of Diocletian - Santa Maria degli Angeli - Santa Maria Maggiore - San Pietro in Vincoli

Colosseum - Arch of Constantine - Domus Aurea - Roman Forum - Palatine Hill - Imperial Fora - Piazza Venezia - Palazzo Venezia - San Marco Evangelista - Victor Emanuel Monument - Capitoline Hill - Palazzo Senatorio, Palazzo Nuovo and Palazzo dei Conservatori - Capitoline Museums - Santa Maria in Aracoeli - Chiesa del Gesù

Basilica dei Santi Apostoli - Piazza and Palazzo del Quirinale - Piazza and Palazzo Barberini - Fontana di Trevi - Via Veneto - Trinità dei Monti - Piazza di Spagna - Piazza del Popolo - Santa Maria del Popolo

Pincio - Villa Medici - Villa Borghese - Galleria Borghese - Galleria Nazionale d'Arte Moderna - Museo Nazionale Etrusco di Villa Giulia

Ara Pacis Agustae - Mausoleum of Augustus - Piazza Colonna - Piazza and Palazzo Montecitorio - Piazza and Church of Sant'Ignazio - Pantheon - Santa Maria sopra Minerva - San Luigi dei Francesi - Palazzo Madama - Piazza Navona - Sant'Agnese in Agone - Sant'Andrea della Valle - Area sacra dell'Argentina - Palazzo Braschi - Museo di Roma - Palazzo della Cancelleria - Campo de' Fiori - Piazza and Palazzo Farnese - Via Giulia - Ponte Sant'Angelo and Castel Sant'Angelo

St. Peter's Square - St. Peter's in the Vatican - Historical Artistic Museum - Treasury of St. Peter's - Vatican Palaces - Vatican Museums - Sistine Chapel - Vatican Gardens

Janiculum - Sant'Onofrio - Tasso's Oak - Beacon of the Janiculum - Piazzale Garibaldi - Villa Doria-Pamphilj - Tempietto of Bramante - Bosco Parrasio - Botanical Gardens - Trastevere - Santa Maria in Trastevere - Santa Cecilia - Palazzo Corsini - Villa Farnesina - Isola Tiberina

Fontana delle Tartarughe - Theatre of Marcellus - Forum Boarium - San Giorgio in Velabro - Santa Maria in Cosmedin - Circus Maximus

Porta San Paolo - Pyramid of Caius Cestius - San Paolo fuori le Mura - Baths of Caracalla - Arch of Druso - Porta San Sebasiano, Museo delle Mura

Via Appia Antica - Catacombs of San Callisto - Catacombs of San Sebastiano - Circus of Maxentius - Tomb of Cecilia Metella - Catacombs of Domitilla

Basilica of San Clemente - Baptistery of San Giovanni in Laterano - Basilica of San Giovanni in Laterano - Palazzo Lateranense - Scala Santa - Basilica of Santa Croce in Gerusalemme

Foro Italico - Ponte Milvio - Auditorium 'Parco della Musica'

Archaeological Museums - Mediaeval and Modern Museums - Military Museums - Religious Museums - Museums of Vatican City

Fresh Tomato bruschetta - Mozzarella in carrozza - Stuffed rice balls - Penne all'arrabbiata - Bucatini alla amatriciana - Linguine with clams - Pasta e ceci - Saltimbocca alla romana - Abbacchio alla cacciatora

HISTORICAL BACKGROUND

The Latin herdsmen from the Alban Hills were the first Italic people to settle on the Palatine Hill, thus beginning the history of Rome. Shortly afterwards they built the Servian Walls to defend themselves from the attacks of the Samnite people from the Tyrrhenian, and of the Etruscans, a civilised race who were soon absorbed by the more warlike people of Rome.

With the foundation of Rome began the splendid adventure of the seven hills, which led to the creation of a great empire, a civilisation which reached to every corner of the known world, the precious remnants of which have survived intact down to our own time.

Caesar, Antony, Octavian Augustus, Nero, Constantine are just some of the characters who, with varying fortunes and great talent, contributed to writing the glorious and eternal history of the "Urbe".

The collapse of the Roman empire coincided with the beginning of a new social configuration which would become a symbol and a guide for the whole world: Christianity, the vibrant power of which is still evident in the mysterious yet evocative catacombs.

Following the advent of Christianity, Rome had been reduced to scarcely thirty thousand inhabitants, scattered between the Pincio, the Tiber and the Capitoline. It was in the 15th century that the urban revival of the Eternal City began, thanks above all to such outstanding popes as Martin V, Nicholas V, Sixtus IV, Julius II and Sixtus V.

This revival continued during the 1500s and the 1600s, thanks also to certain world-famous artists: Michelangelo, Bramante, Raphael, Caravaggio and others, who with their artistic genius helped to restore the city to its ancient splendour.

Finally, in the 1800s, Rome became the capital city of Italy and with that position further augmented its already imposing urban structures.

The rest is the history of the modern day, a history that Rome has managed to immortalise not only through its monuments but also with a social-cultural life which is point of reference and a beacon for all humanity.

APPARTAMENTO DEI CONSERVATORI, CAVALIER D'ARPINO, DISCOVERY OF THE SHE-WOLF, DETAIL

Itinerary no. 1

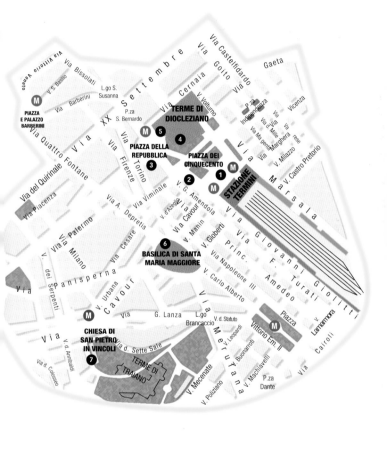

8

9

10

1

O ur itinerary begins from **Piazza dei Cinquecento**, which takes its name from the 500 Italian soldiers who died at Dogali in 1887. The remains of the Servian Walls - built in the year 380 BC to defend Rome from the Gallic Senones people - are still visible in the square where they provide a contrast with the modern Termini station. Overlooking the piazza is **Palazzo Massimo** which (along with Palazzo Altemps, the nearby Baths of Diocletian, the Aula Ottagona or Octagonal Hall, and the Crypta Balbi) is one of the sites of the **Museo Nazionale Romano**. The building houses a numismatic section and a jewellery section containing jewels and gemstones mostly from grave goods; outstanding among them is that of the *Girl of Grottarossa*. It also houses such masterpieces of classical sculpture as the *Niobid of the Gardens of Sallust*, and the *bronze boxer*, as well as various Roman copies of Greek sculptures such as the famous *Lancellotti Discobolus*.

Not far distant is **Piazza della Repubblica**, formerly known as piazza dell'Esedra, embellished with the central Fontana delle Naiadi, the most beautiful modern fountain in Rome, the work of Alessandro Guerrieri, with statues by Mario Rutelli (1901).

Next to the square are the **Baths of Diocletian**, commissioned by the emperor himself and built between 296 and 306 AD. They were the largest baths of ancient Rome. Today parts of the original structure are used to house both the basilica of **Santa Maria degli Angeli** and one of the sites of the Museo Nazionale Romano. The basilica is located in the hall of what used to be the *tepidarium*; Michelangelo adapted it for the church in 1563 and Luigi Vanvitelli restored it in 1749. The external facade is of brickwork and has an elaborate portal. The interior, in the form of a Greek cross, has a large vestibule and eight original red-granite columns supporting the dome.

Among the numerous seventeenth- and eighteenth-century paintings it contains is the *Martyrdom of St. Sebastian* by Domenichino, which used to be in St. Peter's Basilica.

12

In the site of the Museo Nazionale Romano at the Baths it is possible to admire the elegant Great Cloister, attributed to Michelangelo but probably the work of his disciple Jacopo Del Duca, the Ludovisi Cloister and the Giardino dei Cinquecento, chiefly used to house the epigraphic and proto-historical sections of the museum.

Going down via Nazionale and turning left along via Torino we reach the basilica of **Santa Maria Maggiore**, the biggest shrine in Rome to be dedicated to the Virgin Mary. This is one of the four papal basilicas (the others being St. Peter's in the Vatican, San Paolo fuori le Mura and San Giovanni in Laterano); it was built by Sixtus III following the Council of Ephesus in 431, but numerous modern restorations are evident on the exterior. Important features include the thirteenth-century mosaics decorating the mediaeval facade under the loggia, and the Romanesque campanile from 1337 which, at 75 m, is the highest in Rome.

The interior has a nave and two side aisles decorated with gold and marble. Giuliano da Sangallo decorated the coffered wooden ceiling at the end of the 1400s, while the great apse mosaic depicting the *Triumph of Mary* is the work of Jacopo Torriti from 1295. Each of the side aisles opens onto a chapel, both decorated with elegant domes. To the right is the Sistine Chapel, built in honour of Sixtus V by Domenico Fontana in 1585, it houses an important nativity scene sculpted by Arnolfo di Cambio (thirteenth century) located under the central altar. In the left aisle is the Pauline or Borghese Chapel, commissioned by Paul V and built by Flaminio Ponzio; next to that is the Sforza Chapel, built by Giacomo Della Porta to a design by Michelangelo.

17

Santa Maria Maggiore, facade
Santa Maria Maggiore, counter-facade
Santa Maria Maggiore, Jacopo Torriti, *Triumph of Mary*, detail
Piazza Santa Maria Maggiore, column from the basilica of Maxentius with the statue of the *Virgin*
Santa Maria Maggiore, Ferdinando Fuga, baldachin

Proceeding along via Cavour we come to the basilica of **San Pietro in Vincoli**, so-called because it holds the chains used to imprison the Apostle. Built in the fifth century by the empress Eudoxia, it was restored in 1475 by order of Cardinal Giuliano della Rovere, the future Julius II, and again by Francesco Fontana at the beginning of the eighteenth century. The interior, with a nave and two side aisles divided by a series of *spolia* columns, contains one of the most famous Italian works of art: the mausoleum of *Julius II*, commissioned by that pope from Michelangelo for the Vatican Basilica but uncompleted because of the pontiff's death. The *Moses* (1513), with its rich plasticism and constrained energy, is the only sculpture on the monument that can definitely be attributed to Michelangelo. As for the many paintings in the building, they have been attributed to Domenichino, Guercino and Bregno.

18 SAN PIETRO IN VINCOLI, MICHELANGELO, MAUSOLEUM OF *JULIUS II*

19 SAN PIETRO IN VINCOLI, MICHELANGELO, *MOSES*

1

2

3

4

5

6

Itinerary no. 2

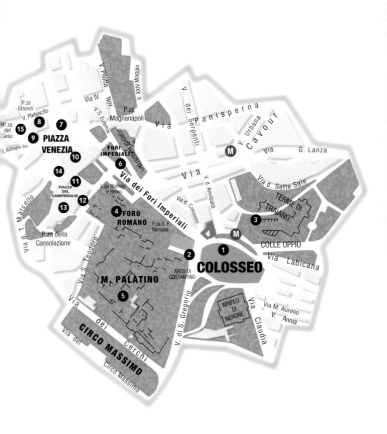

●	Colosseum	❾	San Marco Evangelista
●	Arch of Constantine	❿	Victor Emanuel Monument
●	Domus Aurea	⓫	Capitoline Hill
●	Roman Forum	⓬	Palazzo Senatorio, Palazzo Nuovo
●	Palatine Hill		and Palazzo dei Conservatori
❻	Imperial Fora	⓭	Capitoline Museums
❼	Piazza Venezia	⓮	Santa Maria in Aracoeli
❽	Palazzo Venezia	⓯	Chiesa del Gesù

Via degli Annibaldi leads us to the legendary **Colosseum**, a symbol of the eternity of the Rome and, perhaps, the most famous monument in the world. Its correct name is the Flavian Amphitheatre because work on the structure was begun in the year 72 AD by Vespasian, who was a member of the Flavian Dynasty, but it is commonly known as the Colosseum, perhaps because of the colossal statue of the emperor Nero that once stood nearby.

The work was competed by the emperor Titus, who inaugurated the building in 80 AD with magnificent celebrations and a hundred days of games during which 5,000 wild beasts were killed. The Colosseum remains the world's largest amphitheatre. It is around 50 m high and divided into three levels, each having 80 arches, and an attic storey decorated with pilaster strips and 240 projecting corbels. The corbels, each under a hole in the high cornice, were used to hold posts that supported a vast segmented awning protecting spectators from sun and rain. The interior had capacity for 50,000 spectators who came and went by four main gates.

The nearby **Arch of Constantine** is a celebratory monument dedicated by the senate and the people of Rome to the emperor Constantine following his victory over Maxentius at the Battle of the Milvian Bridge on 28 October 312 AD. It took three years to build and is the largest surviving arch in Rome.

The ***Domus Aurea*** (Golden House), on the Esquiline Hill opposite the Colosseum, in Via Labicana, is the vast palace Nero ordered to be built in 64 AD. Later it was interred to enable the construction of the Baths of Trajan above. From what remains today it is still possible to get an idea of the grandeur of the original structure, with its internal stucco decorations and the beautiful paintings which inspired Renaissance artists to creqate the decorative style known as "grotesques".

The **Roman Forum** - crossed by the Via Sacra which led to the

10

11

12

13

Capitoline - may be accessed from the entrance located near the Portico of the Dii Consentes. The portico itself dates from 367 BC and has only nine surviving columns. Next to it is the Temple of Vespasian built by Domitian in 81 AD; only three columns with Corinthian capitals still remain. Of the Temple of Concordia from 370 AD, built to celebrate peace and equality of rights between patricians and plebeians, nothing is left but the outer wall.

Continuing along the Via Sacra, we come to the church of San Giuseppe dei Falegnami, built in 1540 over the remains of the sinister Mamertine Prison. It was in this prison, originally constructed by Servius Tullius, that Jugurtha and Vercingetorix, among others, were executed; according to tradition, it is also the place where Sts. Peter and Paul were imprisoned. The gaol took its name from the god Mars and was perhaps built over a well where prisoners would be thrown down to their deaths.

On the site once occupied by the guardhouse there is now a chapel, built by Pius IX in 1853.

Turning back to the Roman Forum, we come to the Curia, seat of the Roman senate, traditionally said to have been built by King Tullus Hostilius and transformed into a church in 638. On display inside are the *Plutei of Trajan* depicting two episodes from that emperor's life.

In front of the Curia are the *Comitium*, a meeting place for popular assemblies, and the *Lapis Niger* which takes its name from the dark stone slab which, according to tradition, covers the grave of Romulus.

The third-century Arch of Septimius Severus is almost intact, with its three openings divided by elegant columns. To the left are the *Rostra*, raised tribunes from which orators would address the crowds.

In front of the *Rostra* is the Column of Phocas from 608 AD, the last monument to be built in the Roman Forum.

On the other side of the Via Sacra is the Basilica Julia, built by Julius Caesar in 54 BC as a hall of justice. The Temple of Saturn from 497 BC, on the other hand, was used as the State treasury. It has eight fine columns with Ionic capitals. The nearby Temple of Castor and Pollux from 484 BC has three elegant Corinthian columns.

Proceeding further, we come to the Temple of Julius Caesar, where Caesar was cremated in 44 BC. Next along are the Arch of Augustus, the Fountain of Juturna, the Oratory of the Forty Martyrs, and the church of Santa Maria Antiqua which stands over an old pagan temple and has frescoes dating from the sixth to the eighth century. Near the Arch of Augustus are the remains of the *Regia*, the former archives of State which also held Tacitus' famous Annals; it is said that it was also once the residence of Numa Pompilius. In front of the Regia is the Temple of Vesta and next to that the House of the Vestals, young virgins whose job it was to keep the sacred fire burning in the temple, a symbol of the inextinguishable life of Rome.

The Temple of Antoninus and Faustina from 141 AD, also located on the Via Sacra, was dedicated to the emperor Antoninus Pius and to his wife. Later it became the church of San Lorenzo in Miranda. It still has ten original monolithic columns standing in front of the seventeenth-century facade. Further along the Via Sacra, on the left, is the Temple of Romulus, a circular edifice with a fine bronze door which still has its original lock. It was begun by Maxentius in 308 and dedicated to his son Romulus who died in childhood. In 527 the temple was used as the pronaos of the basilica of Santi Cosma e Damiano, which Pope Felix IV had built in the cella of the

TEMPLE OF SATURN
ARCH OF SEPTIMIUS
SEVERUS
TEMPLE OF
ANTONINUS AND
FAUSTINA AND
SAN LORENZO IN
MIRANDA
HOUSE OF THE
VESTALS

15

16

Templum Sacrae Urbis (or *Bibliotheca Pacis*). The church contains sixth-century mosaics and Baroque decorations.

And it is to Maxentius that another grandiose basilica is dedicated. Once used to administer justice, it was begun in 308 and completed by Constantine in 312 but nothing now remains save a single side aisle with vaults 25 m high (the vaults of the nave were at least 35 m high) which draw attention to the magnificent coffered ceiling. The basilica, which is used for concerts in the summer, has another entrance from Via dei Fori Imperiali.

The Via Sacra ends at the Arch of Titus, commemorating that emperor's conquest of Jerusalem. It has graceful bas-reliefs with scenes of Titus' victories and a single grandiose opening flanked by slim semi-columns with fluting and entablatures.

The **Palatine Hill**, which rises between the Roman Forum and the Circus Maximus, is covered with grandiose imperial palaces. It was chosen as a residence by Augustus, who ordered a complex of buildings to be raised there. The emperor Tiberius, not considering the House of Augustus sufficient for his needs, built another more worthy of his rank, the *Domus Tiberiana* the remains of which are still visible today. During the Middle Ages, the noble Frangipane family took the *Domus* as their residence. Later, in the 1500s, the Farense family ordered the construction of a sumptuous villa of which the Farnese Gardens still remain today as testimony of the decorative tastes of the sixteenth century.

The *Magna Mater* or Temple of Cybele is a group of archaic constructions dating from 204 BC, the most important of which is the one believed to have been the house of Romulus. The House of Livia, on the other hand, was the residence of Augustus' wife and, perhaps, the emperor himself; it is considered to be a classic example of a Roman patrician dwelling being composed of a *Triclinium* and a *Tablinum* (waiting room), decorated with numerous paintings from the first century AD.

The underground cryptoporticus (or gallery), located next to the *Domus Tiberiana*, leads to the *Domus Flavia* which was built by Domitian in the first century AD and includes the basilica for the emperor's audiences and speeches, the throne room (which gives access to the peristyle and the imperial *triclinium*) and the emperor's private apartments.

The *Domus Augustana*, built by Domitian, was the customary dwelling place of that emperor, while the stadium, also the work of Domitian, covered a vast area (160 x 80 m) enclosed by a portico over which stood the imperial tribune. The Baths of Septimius Severus were built next to the palace as is evident from the apses and the bathing halls which still have the original heating systems.

Walking down Via dei Fori Imperiali with our backs to the Colosseum we come to the **Imperial Fora**, built to augment the old Roman Forum which had become too small. Julius Caesar was the first to build a new square (or forum), later followed by Augustus and Nerva, and by Trajan who built the biggest and most prestigious forum of all, 300 m long and 185 m wide. Inaugurated on 12 May 113 AD, it was designed by Apollodorus of Damascus and one may still admire Trajan's Column, 40 m high and resting on a square base of 5 m; it celebrates Trajan's victory over the Dacians in a motif that winds up the column in 23 spirals. The statue of the emperor that once graced the top of the column was replaced by Pope Sixtus V with one of *St. Peter*.

To the right of Trajan's Forum, Trajan's Markets provide testimony of the

BASILICA OF
MAXENTIUS
STADIUM OF
DOMITIAN
PALATINE HILL

scale of Apollodorus' ancient design, even though the majestic House of the Knights of Rhodes was built over the remains in the twelfth century.

Via dei Fori Imperiali, built during the Fascist period to create a triumphal way linking the Colosseum to Piazza Venezia, the fulcrum of the regime's power, divides the Imperial Fora in two. With our backs to the square, on the right is the Forum of Caesar with the Temple of Venus Genetrix and its fine Corinthian columns, reconstructed by Trajan in the second century AD.

The next is the Forum of Augustus, on the opposite side of the road. It was built after the battle of Philippi (42 BC), when Augustus defeated Brutus and Cassius, the assassins of Caesar. Of the few remains still visible today the most noteworthy is the Temple of Mars Ultor

Of the Forum of Nerva (96 AD) all that is left are a few columns (known as *colonnacce*) topped with an interesting frieze.

Near the basilica of Maxentius is a gate leading to the church of Santa Francesca Romana, or Santa Maria Nova, founded in the 900s but completely rebuilt over the following centuries, apart from the bell tower. The interior contains works from the twelfth and thirteenth centuries and a beautiful Cosmatesque floor which gives a great sensation of space. The nearby convent gives access to the *Antiquarium* of the Forum where numerous exhibits from the Imperial Fora may be admired. The building also gives onto the Temple of Venus and Rome, built by the emperor Hadrian in 135 AD.

Piazza Venezia, located almost at the very centre of Rome as many of the city's main thoroughfares start here, takes its name from **Palazzo Venezia**, a splendid example of Renaissance architecture which was ordered to be built by Cardinal Pietro Barbo (the future Pope Paul II) in 1455. The building was first a papal residence, then the headquarters of the Venetian embassy (whence its name) and finally, in 1797, site of the Austrian embassy, before becoming the property of the Italian State. Today it is a museum holding works from various periods and sources, the most important of which are the fourteenth-century *Triptych of Alba Fucens*, the *Head of Christ* by Benozzo Gozzoli, an *Angel with a Scroll* by Bernini, some paintings by Guercino, and tapestries, arms, majolica, silverware, hangings, rings, eighteenth-century fans and crucifixes.

To the left of Palazzo Venezia is the basilica of **San Marco Evangelista**, built in the fourth century AD and restored on a number of occasions by various artists. The facade is probably the work of Alberti, while the portico has been attributed to Maiano.

The interior has many Baroque decorations, the coffered ceiling is a fine Renaissance work, the apse is decorated with splendid eleventh-century mosaics and the sacristy has a fine tabernacle by Mino da Fiesole.

At the far end of Piazza Venezia, at the base of the Capitoline

AERIAL VIEW OF
THE IMPERIAL FORA
TRAJAN'S COLUMN
TRAJAN'S COLUMN,
DETAIL
TRAJAN'S MARKETS

Hill, is the imposing outline of the *Vittoriano*, or **Victor Emanuel Monument**, built by Giuseppe Sacconi between the nineteenth and twentieth centuries to celebrate the unity of Italy.

It is a Neo-classical structure with narrow columns, trophies, allegorical groups and bas-reliefs evoking the ancient Roman style. Also known as the Altar of the Nation, it contains the *Grave of the Unknown Soldier*, an unidentified combatant who fell during the First World War (1915-1918). The fountains to either side symbolise the *Triumphant Love of Homeland*, to the left, and the *Triumph of Work*. Statues over the portico symbolise the *Regions of Italy* while the two chariots on the top represent *Liberty* and the *Unity of Italy*. The entire structure is dominated by the equestrian statue of *Victor Emanuel II*, king of Italy, a work by Enrico Chiaradia, completed by Emilio Gallori. Inside the building are the library, museum and historical institute of the Italian *Risorgimento*.

To the right of the *Vittoriano* is the **Capitoline Hill**, the smallest of the seven hills of Rome and ever an important religious and political centre. Access to the Hill is by the monumental ramp, or *cordonata*, designed by Michelangelo in 1536 and adorned with great statues and trophies: at the base are two Egyptian lions, halfway up on the left is the monument to *Cola di Rienzo* by Girolamo Masini (1887), and at the top are statues of the *Dioscuri* (the twins Castor and Pollux), and a number of ancient sculptures collectively known as the *Trophies of Marius*.

Piazza del Campidoglio, commissioned by Paul III (Alessandro Farnese) and designed by Michelangelo, is an extraordinary example of the harmonious use of light and proportion. Palazzo dei Conservatori to the right and Palazzo Nuovo to the left, their facades decorated with pilaster strips, act as frame to the famous Palazzo Senatorio, headquarters of the local city authorities. All three buildings, which we will examine separately, were constructed to designs by Michelangelo. Palazzo Senatorio and Palazzo dei Conservatori are the work of Giacomo Della Porta in the second half of the sixteenth century, while Palazzo Nuovo was built by Girolamo and Carlo Rainaldi during the seventeenth century. The magnificent statute of *Marcus Aurelius* on horseback, the only equestrian statue to survive from imperial times (second century AD), was brought here in 1538 from its previous location in Piazza del Laterano. The original is now carefully conserved in the new exedra, purpose built by the architect Carlo Aymonino inside Palazzo dei Conservatori to save it from the elements. It's place in the square is taken by a faithful copy.

At the base of the elegant **Palazzo Senatorio** is a fountain with a statue of the goddess *Rome*, ordered to be put there by Michelangelo. The two figures on either side represent the *Nile* and the *Tiber*. Over the palazzo is the Capitoline Tower from the 1500s, with the *Patarina* bell which only rings out on important occasions. Inside the building is the *Aula Consigliare*, also known as the Hall of Julius Caesar as it contains a statue of him dating from 150 AD.

Palazzo Nuovo and Palazzo dei Conservatori are occupied by the **Capitoline Museums**. The collections began with the donation by Pope Sixtus IV (Francesco della Rovere) in 1471 of four famous bronzes: the *Capitoline She-Wolf*, the *Spinario*, the *Camillo*, and the *head*, *hand* and *orb* of the colossal bronze statue of Constantine.

2 AERIAL VIEW OF THE VICTOR EMANUEL MONUMENT, SANTA MARIA IN ARACOELI AND THE CAPITOLINE HILL

3 VICTOR EMANUEL MONUMENT, ENRICO CHIARADIA AND EMILIO GALLORI, EQUESTRIAN STATUE OF *VICTOR EMANUEL II*

4 SAN MARCO EVANGELISTA, INTERIOR

PAGES 28-29, VIEWS THE CAPITOLINE HILL

25

26

Palazzo Nuovo, which also houses part of the Capitoline Museums, contains various important sculptures including, in the courtyard, the gigantic statue of *Marforio* (first century). Among the works held in the upper rooms, the most significant are: the *Dying Gaul* in the Sala del Gladiatore, magnificent Roman copy of a famous Greek sculpture dating from 200 BC, an outstanding example of the harmony of plasticity and expression; a fine pair of *Centaurs* (in the Salone); the 69 busts and hermae in the Sala dei Filosofi portraying poets and rhetoricians from the classical and Hellenistic periods of ancient Greece, and the numerous busts of Roman emperors in the Sala degli Imperatori. The Gabinetto della Venere, with a statue of Venus (copy of a Greek original from the fourth century BC), gives access to the Sala delle Colombe which takes its name from a mosaic of four doves discovered at Hadrian's Villa. In the Sala del Fauno is a beautiful red-marble statue of the *Laughing Silenus*, a second-century AD copy of a late Hellenistic original.

The Capitoline Museum collections continue in **Palazzo dei Conservatori** with the Appartamento dei Conservatori and the Capitoline Pinacoteca. Access to the Appartamento is across a courtyard with a fine portico containing archaeological exhibits including the gigantic remains of a 12 m high marble statue of *Constantine*. The stairs leading to the upper floors are decorated with reliefs from a late-imperial monument honouring Marcus Aurelius. At the top are the rooms dedicated to the Horti Romani, with fine sculptures and exhibits found in the gardens of the Esquiline, and the exedra of Marcus Aurelius which contains the famous Capitoline bronzes and a section dedicated to the Temple of Capitoline Jupiter. The Appartamento dei Conservatori, on the first floor, begins with the Sala degli Orazi e Curiazi frescoed by Cavalier d'Arpino with episodes from Roman history. It contains a marble statue of *Urban VIII* by Bernini and a bronze statue of *Innocent X* by Algardi. The following rooms house some of the most important works in the museum: in the Sala dei Trionfi is the simple yet magnificent *Spinario*, a first-century copy of a Greek original from the fifth century BC depicting a boy removing a thorn from his left foot, and a bronze bust of extraordinary expressive power from the fourth-third century BC called *Capitoline Brutus*; the Sala della Lupa holds the Etruscan statue of the *She-Wolf*, the symbol of Rome to which *Romulus and Remus* were later added, attributed to Pollaiolo. The Pinacoteca Capitolina, founded by Benedict XIV, includes masterpieces by Dossi, Veronese, Guercino, Parmigianino, Tintoretto, Caravaggio, Pietro da Cortona, as well as a splendid collection of porcelain.

EQUESTRIAN STATUE
OF *MARCUS
AURELIUS*
PIAZZA DI
CAMPIDOGLIO,
LEFT-HAND
DIOSCURI
CAPITOLINE
PINACOTECA,
CARAVAGGIO, THE
FORTUNE TELLER

The church of **Santa Maria in Aracoeli** was built on the Capitoline in the fourth century. It has had great religious and social importance for the city over the centuries and houses the so-called *Santo Bambino dell'Aracoeli*, a fine seventh-century sculpture of the Baby Jesus made of olive wood from the Garden of Gethsemane. It has been replaced with a copy since it was stolen in 1994.

The exterior facade is square with a rose window to either side while the interior (a nave and side aisles separated by 22 columns) is outstanding for its Cosmatesque floor from the 1200s and the sixteenth century ceiling commemorating the naval battle of Lepanto. To the right of the entrance is the funerary monument of *Cardinal d'Albret*, by Bregno (1400s), and to the left the tomb of *Giovanni Crivelli*, by Donatello. The first chapel in the right aisle has frescoes showing the *Life of St. Bernardino*, by Pinturicchio, while the second to the eighth chapel contain masterpieces dating from the seventeenth to the nineteenth century.

Over the main altar of the presbytery is the *Madonna dell'Aracoeli* to whom the church is dedicated, while in the left transept the Chapel of St. Helena (who rediscovered the True Cross) contains relics of that saint and a monument to *Matteo d'Acquasparta* from the 1300s, a work by Giovanni di Cosma. The fresco above is of the Cavallini school. In the third chapel of the left aisle is St. *Anthony of Padua with two supplicants*, all that remains of the frescoes by Benozzo Gozzoli that once decorated the chapel.

Behind Palazzo Venezia is the **Chiesa del Gesù**, the main Jesuit church in Rome. It was begun by Vignola in 1568, in collaboration with Giacomo Della Porta who modified the facade and designed the dome. The Latin-cross interior has an aisleless nave surrounded by side chapels, with a barely protruding transept and a dome inundated with light. In the left transept is the chapel of St. Ignatius Loyola, founder of the Jesuit Order, who is buried under an altar considered to be one of the richest in the world. The ceiling fresco over the nave represents the *Triumph of the Name of Jesus* and is the work of Gaulli, known as Baciccia, a talented pupil of Bernini (seventeenth century).

31

SANTA MARIA IN
ARACOELI
SANTA MARIA IN
ARACOELI, INTERIOR
SANTA MARIA IN
ARACOELI, WOODEN
CEILING
CAPITOLINE HILL,
EGYPTIAN LION

1

2

3

4

5

6

7

Itinerary no. 3

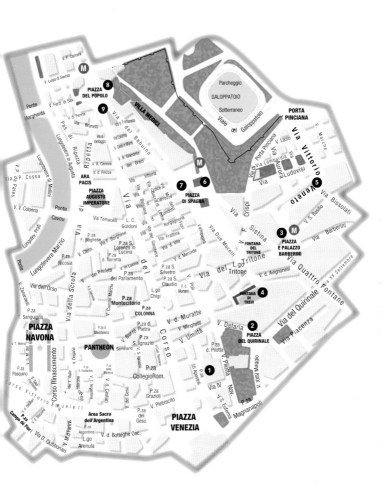

The basilica dei **Santi Apostoli**, in the square of the same name, was erected in the sixth century but almost completely rebuilt by Carlo Fontana in 1714. The facade is the work of Giuseppe Valadier (1827). The fine Renaissance portico by Baccio Pontelli (late fifteenth century) was later transformed by Rainaldi in 1681, it holds the funerary stele of *Giovanni Volpato* by Canova (1807) and an *imperial eagle* from the second century AD.

The interior of the church has a nave and two side aisles separated by pilasters. The central vault was decorated by Baciccia (1707) and the presbytery by Giovanni Odazzi. To the left of the presbytery is the funerary monument of *Cardinal Riario*, the work of Andrea Bregno who also designed the funerary monument of *Raffaele della Rovere* (1477) located in the crypt of the confessio.

At the end of the left aisle is the funerary monument of *Clement XIV*, a masterpiece by Canova (1789).

Piazza del Quirinale, not far from Santi Apostoli, stands on the highest hill of Rome from which it takes its name. The piazza is adorned with the famous statues of the *Dioscuri* (Castor and Pollux), Roman copies of a Greek original dating from the fifth century BC. Behind them is a slim obelisk taken from the Mausoleum of Augustus, and underneath is a fountain.

Palazzo del Quirinale - to the right of which is Palazzo della Consulta, an eighteenth-century work by Fuga - was first the summer residence of the popes, then from 1870 the palace of the kings of Italy and finally, from 1946 to the present, the residence of the president of the Republic. The name derives from that of Quirinus, the god of the Sabines. Work on the building was begun in 1574 by Gregory XIII and came to an end in 1700. The fine exterior portal is by Maderno who also designed the Pauline Chapel inside. The stupendous porticoed courtyard is the work of Domenico Fontana and gives access to a beautiful garden.

Following our route along Via del Quirinale, we come to the church of Sant'Andrea al Quirinale. It dates from 1671 and is by Bernini, one of the artist's most important works, with a curved portico in the facade and an interior that is tiny yet luminous, an effect of its elliptical design. Another noteworthy feature is the dome with its gilded coffers and stuccoes, by Raggi.

Further along is the church of San Carlo alle Quattro Fontane (or San Carlino), Borromini's first commission, which he came to after having worked on the marble of the fabric of St. Peter's. The audacious and original design has an elliptical plan with a facade of two orders and a distinctive campanile. The entrance and the high altar are aligned on the main axis. The dome, also elliptical, uses hexagonal and octagonal coffers to create crosses.

Borromini also participated in the construction of the small but magnificent cloister, beginning in 1667, a true example of Baroque architecture.

At the crossroads of the Quattro Fontane, with its four unexceptional fountains, we turn left towards the nearby **Palazzo Barberini**.

Begun by Maderno and completed by Bernini in 1633, it has a facade of three orders with large windows and classical-style arches. The building houses the Galleria Nazionale d'Arte Antica which includes paintings by Pietro da Cortona, Simone Martini, Fra Angelico, Filippo Lippi (*Annunciation*), Lotto, Sodoma, Raphael (*La Fornarina*), El Greco,

Tintoretto (*Christ and the adulteress*), Titian (*Philip II*), Caravaggio (*Judith and Holofernes*) and Hans Holbein (*Henry VIII*).

A grandiose fresco depicting the *Triumph of Providence*, painted by Pietro da Cortona in 1639, decorates the ceiling of the Salone.

Piazza Barberini is dominated by the Fontana del Tritone, a masterpiece sculpted by Bernini for Pope Urban VIII in 1643. It is characterised by four dolphins with raised tails and by the coat-of-arms of the Barberini family, while astride a great scallop shell the Triton blows into a conch shell and sends a spout of water up into the air.

There is an exact copy of this fountain in Nuremberg.

To the side of the piazza is the Fontana delle Api, created by Bernini in 1644 in honour of Urban VIII.

To visit the monumental **Fontana di Trevi**, commissioned by Pope Clement XII and built by Nicola Salvi, considered the most famous fountain in the world, we must follow Via del Tritone then turn left along Via Poli at the end of which is a truly superb sight: The great central niche in the rear wall of Palazzo Poli is occupied by the mythological god Neptune standing on a chariot drawn by two Tritons in a magically-animated scene of horses, rocks, vegetation and cascades. The magnificent sculptures are the work of Pietro Bracci. The water of the fountain is called *vergine* because the source was revealed to Agrippa's soldiers by a young girl. Completion of the fountain has taken three centuries of restoration and retouches.

Turning back to Piazza Barberini we go up **Via Veneto** which, with its luxury hotels and cafés frequented by stars of stage and screen, is the most famous street in Rome. On the way we pass the seventeenth-century church of Santa Maria della Concezione, which has works by Reni and Domenichino, and underground chapels decorated with the bones of thousands of Capuchin monks. Opposite Palazzo Margherita, once the residence to the queen of that name, we turn into Via Liguria which comes out into Via Sistina. There, visitors may admire the church of **Trinità dei Monti** from which the Spanish Steps (137 steps with alternating ramps and terraces) slope down towards the evocative **Piazza di Spagna**, which takes its name from the palazzo of the old Spanish embassy to the Holy See. The steps were designed by Francesco De Sanctis in the eighteenth century. At the centre of the piazza is the beautiful Fontana della Barcaccia, a work from 1629 by Pietro Bernini, father of the more famous Gian Lorenzo. To the right is the Column of the Immaculate Conception, erected by Pope Pius IX in 1865.

Piazza di Spagna opens onto some of the most well-known streets of Rome, such as Via Condotti with its famous Caffè Greco from the 1700s, Via Margutta, a meeting place for artists, and Via del Babuino which is full of antique shops and leads to **Piazza del Popolo**, a masterpiece of Neo-classical architecture designed by Giuseppe Valadier in the early 1800s.

At the beginning of Via del Corso are the "twin" churches of Santa Maria di Montesanto (1679) and Santa Maria dei Miracoli (1681), built by Carlo Rainaldi and completed by Bernini and Carlo Fontana. Facing them is the Porta del Popolo which opens onto the Via Flaminia and has an austere external facade by Nanni di Baccio Bigio (1565) built to a design by Michelangelo. The facade overlooking Piazza del Popolo, on the other hand, is by Bernini and was completed in 1655 for the arrival in Rome of Queen Christina of Sweden. On the same side of the square is the eleventh-century church of **Santa Maria del Popolo**, erected by Paschal II and rebuilt in the Renaissance by Baccio Pontelli. It has a typical pointed campanile and a characteristic Renaissance interior with a nave and two side aisles, transept and dome. Among the masterpieces it contains are Pinturicchio's frescoes in the presbytery, two tombs by Sansovino on the side-walls of the choir, the Chigi Chapel (second in the left aisle) designed by Raphael, and two famous Caravaggios (in the first chapel of the left arm of the transept), the *Conversion of Saul* and the *Crucifixion of Peter*.

At the centre of Piazza del Popolo is the Flaminio Obelisk, brought from Egypt to Rome by the emperor Augustus and erected in this square during the reign of Sixtus V in a magnificent combination of ancient Egyptian civilisation and imposing Roman remains. Around 24 m high, the monolith has hieroglyphs of Seti (1304 BC) and celebrates the symbol of the sun.

18

SANTA MARIA DI MONTESANTO AND SANTA MARIA DEI MIRACOLI

SANTA MARIA DEL POPOLO, CARAVAGGIO, CONVERSION OF SAUL

SANTA MARIA DEL POPOLO, CARAVAGGIO, CRUCIFIXION OF PETER

PIAZZA DEL POPOLO, FLAMINIO OBELISK

Itinerary no. 4

❶ Pincio

❷ Villa Medici

❸ Villa Borghese

❹ Galleria Borghese

❺ Galleria Nazionale d'Arte Moderna

❻ Museo Nazionale Etrusco
di Villa Giulia

6

The Pincio is a large and famous garden covering the hill of the same name, designed by Valadier at the beginning of the nineteenth century. Once the site of patrician villas, it offers a stupendous view over the city. Before starting down one of its many paths, let us visit **Villa Medici**, built by Annibale Lippi for Cardinal Ricci in the sixteenth century and acquired by the Medici family in the seventeenth century. In 1803 Napoleon made it the French Academy and still today - apart from being home to many classical sculptures - it welcomes French artists who wish to pursue their studies in Rome

Having crossed Piazza di Siena, a picturesque hippodrome surrounded by pine trees, we find ourselves in the heart of **Villa Borghese**, the largest park in Rome and site of the famous Casino Borghese, commissioned by Cardinal Scipione Borghese and built by Jan Van Santen (1616).

The facade of the Casino is decorated with niches enclosing statues from various periods (almost like an open-air art gallery) and with the five arches of the entrance portico which contains sculptures and fragments from Roman times. This is the site of the **Galleria Borghese**, one of the richest private collections in the world. It was brought together by Cardinal Borghese who used all possible means, fair and foul, to get hold of the works it contains, such as tricking the Duke of Ferrara into letting him have the paintings of Dossi, blackmailing his colleague Cardinal Sfondrato to get the works by Titian, or commissioning the night theft of the *Deposition* by Raphael from the Baglioni Chapel in Perugia.

In this magnificent collection, alongside ancient sculptures, we may admire stupendous works by Bernini such as the famous *Rape of Persephone*, in the Sala degli Imperatori. Other equally celebrated pieces include *Apollo and Daphne* and *David*, also by Bernini, and the *Venus Victrix*, a statue by Canova showing Pauline Bonaparte, Napoleon's sister, a widow whose second marriage in 1803 was to Camillo Borghese. The statue immediately became famous for its beauty and Pauline, who soon separated from her husband, sought in vain to gain possession of it.

Noteworthy paintings include the *Deposition* by Raphael, *Boy with a Basket of Fruit*, *Sick Bacchus*, *David with the head of Goliath*, and *St. Jerome*, all by Caravaggio, and masterpieces by Rubens, Titian, Sodoma, Antonello da Messina, Giorgione, Dossi and others.

Other features worthy of attention in Villa Borghese include the

VILLA BORGHESE, NEO-CLASSICAL PROPYLAEA
VIEW OF ROME FROM THE PINCIO
GALLERIA BORGHESE, GIAN LORENZO BERNINI, *APOLLO AND DAPHNE*
MUSEO NAZIONALE ERUSCO DI VILLA GIULIA, *RED-FIGURE ATTIC VASE*
MUSEO NAZIONALE ETRUSCO DI VILLA GIULIA, COURTYARD
VILLA MEDICI
VILLA BORGHESE, CASINO BORGHESE
VILLA BORGHESE, TEMPLE OF AESCULAPIUS
VILLA BORGHESE, WATER CLOCK
VILLA BORGHESE

11

12

13

14

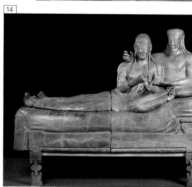

15

Neo-classical propylaea which were built by Luigi Canina in 1825-1830 and form the entrance to the park from Piazzale Flaminio, the Zoo, the Museo Civico di Zoologia, the Orangery (Museo Carlo Bilotti), the Museo Canonica, the lake with its Neo-classical temple by Antonio and Mario Asprucci (1787) dedicated to Aesculapius, the god of medicine, and Valle Giulia with the interesting **Galleria Nazionale d'Arte Moderna** which documents the development of Italian and foreign art from the 1800s to today.

In Villa Giulia, on the other hand, is the **Museo Nazionale Etrusco di Villa Giulia**, a fine museum of the Etruscan period with exhibits displayed in more than 30 rooms. Among the outstanding works it contains is the famous terracotta *Sarcophagus of husband and wife* from the fourth century BC, a *Centaur*, a *Youth astride a Sea-Horse* from the sixth century BC, the magnificent *Apollo and Hercules* of Veio, and an entire Etruscan tomb discovered at Cerveteri.

GALLERIA BORGHESE, CARAVAGGIO, *BOY WITH A BASKET OF FRUIT*

GALLERIA BORGHESE, RAPHAEL, *LADY WITH A UNICORN*

GALLERIA BORGHESE, RAPHAEL, *DEPOSITION*

MUSEO NAZIONALE ETRUSCO DI VILLA GIULIA, *SARCOPHAGUS OF HUSBAND AND WIFE*

GALLERIA BORGHESE, ANTONIO CANOVA, *PAULINE BORGHESE AS VENUS VICTRIX*

MUSEO NAZIONALE ETRUSCO DI VILLA GIULIA, *HERCULES OF VEIO*

MUSEO NAZIONALE ETRUSCO DI VILLA GIULIA

MUSEO NAZIONALE ETRUSCO DI VILLA GIULIA, GOLDEN CROWN WITH PEARLS AND CARNELIANS

18

17

Villa Borghese Gardens

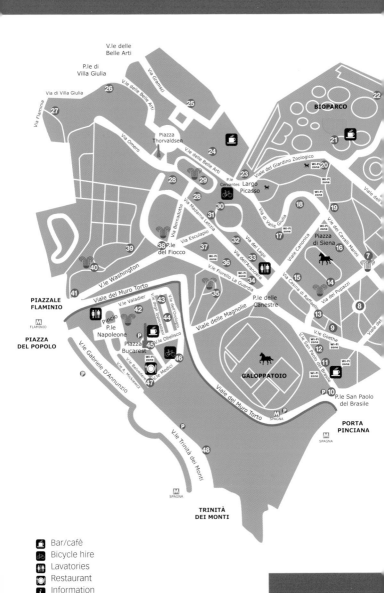

Bar/cafè
Bicycle hire
Lavatories
Restaurant
Information
Fountains
Dog-walking area
Wireless internet access
Underground railway station

Itinerary no. 5

S tarting from Piazza del Popolo, we follow Via di Ripetta to the ***Ara Pacis Augustae***, a famous monument erected by Augustus (9 BC) to celebrate the *Pax Romana* after wars in Gaul and Spain. The altar is protected under a canopy of glass, steel and Tivoli marble which also includes an auditorium and various exhibition halls, the work of the American architect Richard Meier. The marble reliefs around the sides of the altar - symbolising the fruitfulness of the earth, sacrifices, and the imperial court - have a truly vivid and plastic quality.

Next to the *Ara Pacis* is the broad Piazza Augusto Imperatore, at the centre of which is the **Mausoleum of Augustus**, a vast construction 89 m in diameter and with a conical tumulus 44 m high. Here Augustus and other members of the Julio-Claudian dynasty were buried, as evinced by the travertine burial chamber containing cinerary urns. In the Middle Ages, the Colonna family transformed the mausoleum into a fortress. Much later it was used as a concert venue, until 1936 when it was again given over as a tourist site.

The neighbouring church of Santi Ambrogio e Carlo al Corso, built to a design by Martino and Onorio Longhi, has a superb dome by Pietro da Cortona, while the vast Baroque interior contains a majestic altarpiece by Maratta (1690) over the main altar. Giacinto Brandi's frescoes in the nave (*Fall of the Rebel Angels*) and on the ceiling of transept and presbytery (*Glory of St. Charles* and *St. Charles and the Plague Victims*) are likewise not to be missed.

We now follow Via del Corso to **Piazza Colonna**, the hub of metropolitan life. It is flanked by the stupendous Palazzo Chigi, built by Giacomo Della Porta (1562), restored by Carlo Maderno and completed by Felice Della Greca. Today it is the official seat of the Italian prime minister.

At the centre of the piazza stands the Column of Marcus Aurelius, erected in honour of that emperor between 176 and 193 AD. It is 42 m high including the base and decorated with a spiral bas-relief narrating Marcus Aurelius' victories against the Marcomanni (lower half) and the Sarmatians (upper half).

At the top is a statue of St. Paul, put there by Sixtus V in 1589.

To reach **Piazza Montecitorio** we must follow the street running up from Palazzo Chigi. Dominating the piazza is the obelisk of Pius VI, dating from the time of the pharaoh Psammetichus II (594-589 BC) who is depicted as a crouching sphinx while winged scarabs hold up the disc of the sun. The granite obelisk is around 22 m high and was brought to Rome from Heliopolis during the reign of the emperor Augustus.

Palazzo Montecitorio, designed by Bernini in 1650 on the orders of Innocent X, was completed by Carlo Fontana in 1694. Since 1871 it has been the seat of the Italian Chamber of Deputies.

Crossing Piazza di Pietra, we come to **Piazza Sant'Ignazio** with the **church** of the same name, begun by Orazio Grassi in 1626 under the supervision of Carlo Maderno, Orazio Torriani and Paolo Marucelli. The interior, with a nave and side aisles, celebrates the figure of St. Ignatius Loyola and is decorated with marble and frescoes, such as the marble high-relief by Pierre Legros (seventeenth century) showing the *Glory of St. Luigi Gonzaga* (altar in the right transept), and the famous ceiling fresco of the *Triumph of St. Ignatius*, a magnificent achievement of perspective by Andrea Pozzo.

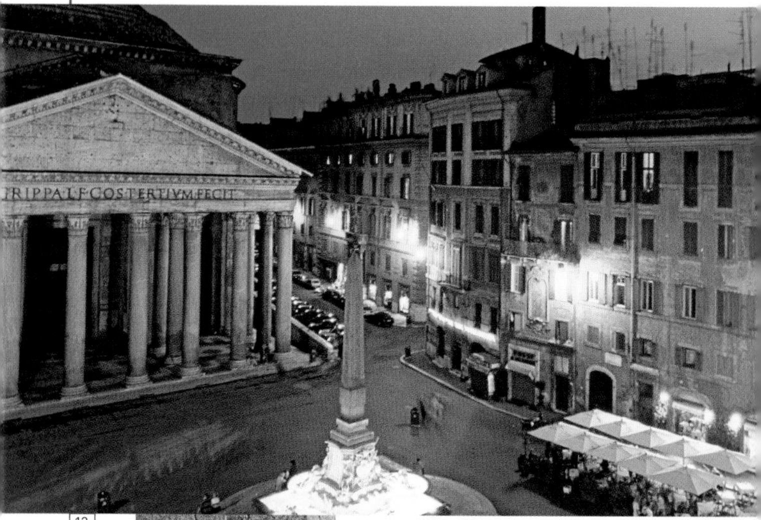

12

13

14

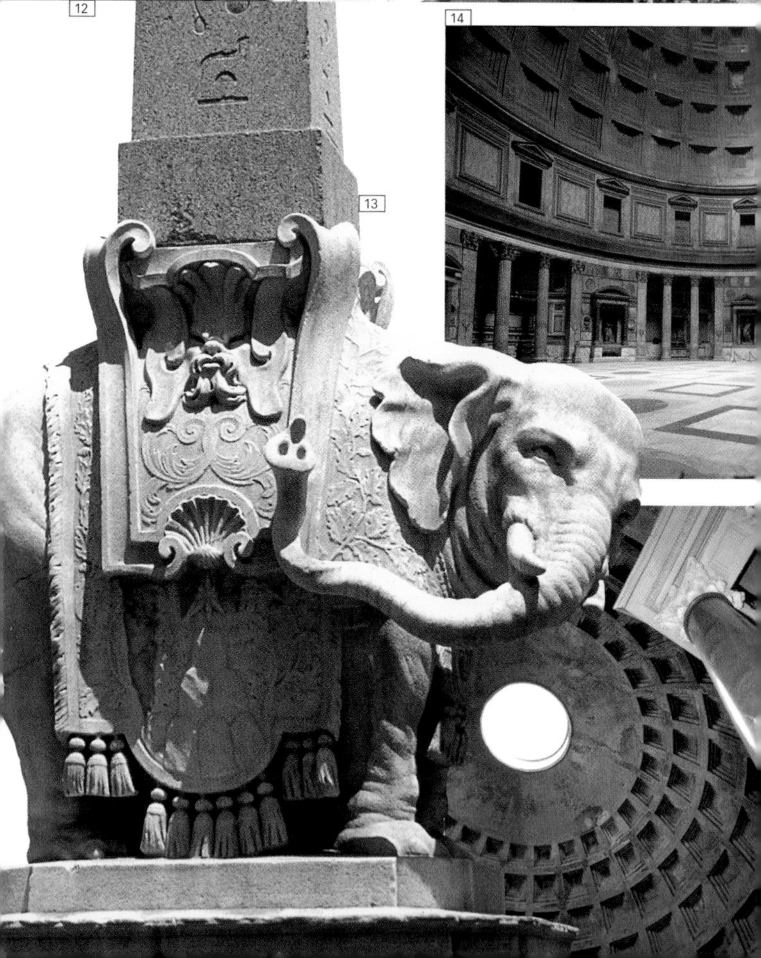

Via del Seminario leads to Piazza della Rotonda and the famous **Pantheon,** in front of which is an obelisk, almost complete, of Ramesses II from Heliopolis. It is 6.34 m high and stands over a fountain built by Giacomo Della Porta (1578).

The Pantheon is one of the best-known monuments of Roman art. It was built by Marcus Agrippa in 27 BC as evinced by the inscription on the architrave, and its name means "monument dedicated to all the gods". Restored by Diocletian in 80 AD and rebuilt by Hadrian, it is one of the best preserved of its kind in the world. Both the dome and the bronze doors (138 AD) date from the Roman period. In Christian times, the Pantheon was transformed into a church. The construction is made up of a massive coffered cylinder over which sits a broad dome of 43.3 metres with a central oculus to admit the light.

The exterior has a pronaos with sixteen 12.5 m high columns and a great tympanum. The circular interior is adorned with seven large semicircular and rectangular niches, and eight aedicules. The second niche on the right contains the tomb of king *Vittorio Emanuele II*, and the third on the left that of king *Umberto I* and of queen *Margherita*, while the third aedicule on the left houses the tomb of the painter Raphael Sanzio (1520), buried here at his own express wish.

From the Pantheon a short walk takes us to Piazza della Minerva with its small red granite obelisk (5.47 m). The obelisk is dedicated to the pharaoh Apries (539-570 BC) and is decorated with his hieroglyphics. The *elefantino* (called *pulcino* by the Romans) supporting the obelisk was designed by Bernini and sculpted by Ercole Ferrata. The presence of the elephant counterpoises the metaphorical significance of the pachyderm (strong and balanced) with the sense of ancient wisdom symbolised by the obelisk. The church of **Santa Maria sopra Minerva** was constructed in 1280 over the ruins of a temple dedicated to Minerva Calcidica. The facade by Meo del Caprino (1453) has three Renaissance portals, while the interior with a nave and two aisles is the only example of Gothic architecture in Rome.

The church contains many works of art: the *Risen Christ*, a famous sculpture by Michelangelo (1521) to the left of the main altar; the Carafa Chapel with magnificent frescoes by Filippino Lippi (1489); the tombs of *Leo X* and *Clement VII* by Antonio da Sangallo the Younger, behind the main altar; a funerary monument by Bernini in the left aisle, and the tomb of *Fra Angelico* located in the first chapel of the left transept. Other works of lesser artistic value are nonetheless worth seeing.

From the Pantheon, passing down Via Giustiniani we come to the church of **San Luigi dei Francesi**, dating from the sixteenth century and attributed to Giacomo Della Porta and Domenico Fontana.

The interior was restored by Dérizet in 1764. The fifth chapel on the left contains three famous chiaroscuro masterpieces by the artistic genius Caravaggio (1597): *St. Matthew and the Angel*, the *Calling of St. Matthew*, and the *Martyrdom of St. Matthew*.

Equally important are Domenichino's frescoes in the second chapel on the right, showing scenes from the *Life of St. Cecilia*.

Palazzo Madama, located in Piazza Madama, was built by the Medici in the sixteenth century and takes its name from Margherita d'Austria, wife of Alessandro de' Medici and daughter of Charles V. The majestic Baroque facade by Cigoli and Marinelli has a fine portal with two columns and four rows of windows.

16

17

18

19

20

The building is the seat of the Italian Senate and contains a large library. Overlooking Piazza Sant'Apollinare is the splendid **Palazzo Altemps**, one of the locations of the **Museo Nazionale Romano**, which houses important collections of ancient sculptures. Of particular value are the works of the Boncompagni Ludovisi collection, including: the *Gaul committing suicide with his wife* from the first century AD; the *Ludovisi Throne*, a magnificent piece from the fifth century BC portraying the birth of Venus, and the *Ludovisi Ares*, a copy of an original by Lysippos.

Piazza Navona, the most typical Baroque square in Rome, stands on the ruins of the stadium of Domitian (276 x 54 m) and is graced with three breathtaking fountains. At the centre of the piazza is the famous Fontana dei Fiumi, a work by Bernini who "stole" the commission from Borromini, submitting his own design to Pope Innocent X with the collusion of Donna Olimpia, the pontiff's influential sister-in-law. The fountain is a magnificent portrayal of the four main rivers of the world: Nile, Ganges, Danube and Plate, representing the four continents then known.

Above the fountain is a 16.53 m high granite obelisk decorated with hieroglyphics representing the gods of Egypt and the glory of the emperor Domitian (81-96 AD).

The monument, completed in 1651, also includes the biblical message of the dove bearing an olive branch (the symbol of the Pamphilj family), which sealed the pact between God and mankind after the Great Flood. The Fontana del Moro, designed by Bernini, was constructed by Mari (seventeenth century). It stands in front of Palazzo Pamphilj (seat of the Brazilian embassy) which was given by Innocent X to Donna Olimpia and boasts a gallery frescoed in 1654 by Pietro da Cortona.

Lastly, the Fontana del Nettuno was built by Della Porta in 1576 but subsequently modified. The basin, in fact, is from the 1500s while the statues date from 1873.

Facing Bernini's central fountain is the church of **Sant'Agnese in Agone**, which takes its name from the word "agones", a reference to the games that took place in the piazza in antiquity.

According to tradition, it was on the site of the church that St. Agnes was forced to strip naked before the populace, whereupon her hair miraculously grew to cover her. Building work began in 1652 under the supervision of Girolamo and Carlo Rainaldi, and was completed in 1657 by Borromini who also designed the twin campaniles. The Greek-cross interior shows an interesting use of chiaroscuro and has rich marble altarpieces by various artists (Caffà, Guidi). The dome, frescoed by Ferri, rests on eight columns by Baciccia. Remains of the stadium of Domitian are still visible in the crypt.

From Piazza Navona, across Corso Vittorio Emanuele II, is the majestic dome of **Sant'Andrea della Valle**, the third biggest in Rome after St. Peter's and the Pantheon. Work began in 1591 to a design by Pietro Paolo Olivieri, then restarted under the guidance of Maderno in 1608. The church was consecrated in 1650. The interior, with an aisleless nave and side chapels, is very spacious and full of light, thanks especially to the broad barrel-vaulted ceiling and the enormous apse. It contains some important works of art, such as bronze copies of *Rachel* and *Leah*, and of Michelangelo's *Pietà* in the second chapel on the right. Also worthy of note are the tombs of *Pius II* (by a follower of Andrea Bregno, 1475) and *Pius III* (Sebastiano Ferrucci, 1503), over the

entrances to the circular chapels. The dome was frescoed by Lanfranco, while the *Evangelists* in the pendentives and the frescoes in the apse are by Domenichino (1628).

In Largo di Torre Argentina is an archaeological site known as the **area sacra dell'Argentina**, with four temples of uncertain identification. The first (from the third century BC) is also the best preserved having been partially transformed into a church in the Middle Ages. The second, a round temple, was probably dedicated to Fortuna in 101 BC. The third is the oldest (early third century BC) and reveals Etruscan-Italic construction styles, while the fourth (dating from the second century BC) is more striking than the others because, being built in the Republican age, it is made of travertine,.

Along Corso Vittorio Emanuele II is Piazza San Pantaleo, which takes its name from the eighteenth-century church with a facade by Valadier (1806). Overlooking the square is **Palazzo Braschi**, built by Cosimo Morelli in 1792 for the nephews of Pius VI (Giovanni Angelo Braschi). The building has a second entrance on Via di Pasquino, so-called for the Hellenistic statue it contains, used to append satirical attacks against the papal authorities.

Palazzo Braschi is the site of the **Museo di Roma**, which contains a great variety of exhibits relating to the history of the city from the Middle Ages to the mid 1900s, including furniture, carriages, elements of architectural and urban decor, mosaics and frescoes salvaged from demolition, mediaeval ceramics, and wooden stamps for textile manufacture in the 1700s and 1800s. The art gallery is particularly important, with works by Andrea Sacchi, Pierre Subleyras, Pier Leone Ghezzi, Marco Benefial and Pompeo Batoni. Also worthy of note is the collection of sculptures, from the Middle Ages to the nineteenth century, which illustrates the work of some of the most important sculptors active in Rome: Francesco Mochi, Alessandro Algardi and Pietro Tenerani.

Palazzo della Cancelleria in the piazza of the same name was begun by 1453 and completed by Bramante in 1511. The interior contains the Sala Riaria, the Salone dei Cento Giorni and the magnificent three-storey courtyard, one of the highest expressions of Renaissance art.

A short walk takes us to **Campo de' Fiori** which owes is name to the vast field that covered this area in the Middle Ages, used as site for the public execution of criminals and heretics, as evinced by the statue of *Giordano Bruno* burnt alive here on 17 February 1600. A picturesque local fruit and vegetable market is set up in the piazza every day.

Behind Campo de' Fiori is Piazza Farnese with its twin fountains with large granite basins. Here is the most beautiful Renaissance building in Rome, **Palazzo Farnese**, site of the French embassy to Italy. It was begun in 1514 by Antonio da Sangallo the Younger for Cardinal Farnese (the future Paul Paolo III) and continued by Michelangelo, who added the balcony, the cornice with its Farnese lilies and the second floor of the courtyard (1546). The palazzo was completed by Giacomo Della Porta in 1589.

Inside is the sublime atrium by Sangallo, with three naves and granite columns. This leads into the courtyard and then on to the first floor where visitors can admire the gallery with its famous frescoes by Carracci and his disciples (1597-1604).

27

28

Via Giulia, with its antique shops, its art galleries and its palazzos, is the world's most famous sixteenth-century street. So famous was it that it used to be described as the parlour of Rome, a title since acquired by Via Veneto.

From Via Giulia, having traversed Via Banco di Santo Spirito, we come to **Ponte Sant'Angelo**, formerly known as *Ponte Elio*, the most outstanding of the ancient bridges of Rome, evocatively framed by the ten statues placed here in the 1600s to symbolise the Passion of Christ.

At the other end of the bridge stands **Castel Sant'Angelo** in all its austere beauty, a grandiose tomb built by the emperor Hadrian for himself, completed by the architect Demetrianus in 130. The angel's place at the top of the structure was once occupied by a statue of the emperor, but in 590 an angel appearing to Pope Gregory the Great brought an end to an outbreak of the plague, a statue of the angel was raised and the mausoleum became known as Castel Sant'Angelo.

Access to the castle is by the Cortile del Salvatore. From there a vast ramp passes up through the burial chamber and leads to the Cortile dell'Angelo, which takes its name from the enormous angel by Raffaello da Montelupo which stood over the castle from the 1500s to the 1700s. The courtyard is also called "delle Palle" because of the cannonballs piled there. In any case, its most important feature is the double row of windows at the end, the work of Michelangelo (1514).

The courtyard gives access to other rooms with magnificent ceilings, finally leading to the third floor and the Cortile di Alessandro VI, with its magnificent well decorated with the coat-of-arms of the Borgia family. From here a short flight of stairs leads up to the Bathroom of Clement VII (Giulio de' Medici), decorated by Giulio Romano who took as his model the rooms frescoed by Raphael in the Vatican Palaces. The small space is decorated with grotesques and still has the two conduits that brought hot and cold water to the marble tub. In order to make the room more comfortable, cavity walls were built so the interior could be heated by the passage of hot air.

Be sure to visit the historical prisons - known as Bocca dell'Inferno (Mouth of Hell) - where, among others, Cellini (who escaped), Giordano Bruno, Cagliostro and various figures of the Italian Risorgimento were all imprisoned.

At the south end of the castle is the Loggia di Giulio II by Bramante, and the Sala del Perseo which takes its name from a painted frieze of Perseus running along the top of the wall. It is a sixteenth-century work by Perin del Vaga who also decorated the Sala Paolina and the Sala di Amore e Psiche. Further along is the Camera del Tesoro and the well-stocked Library which, like the preceding rooms, are all part of the Apartments of Paul III, with frescoes and grotesques by Luzio Luzzi and stuccowork from the 1500s. The Library gives access to the upper terrace whence it is possible to admire the bronze angel by Pieter Anton van Verschaffelt from 1753, and a splendid panoramic view over the city. A final interesting detail is that behind an iron grating on one of the bastions is a passage running atop the Leonine Walls along which popes could secretly reach Vatican City. Nicholas II designed it in 1277-1280 and Pope Clement VII used it when the Lanszknechts descended upon Rome in 1527, looting and terrorising the entire city.

29

AERIAL VIEW
OF PONTE
SANT'ANGELO
AND CASTEL
SANT'ANGELO

CASTEL
SANT'ANGELO,
SALA PAOLINA

CASTEL
SANT'ANGELO,
CORTILE
DELL'ANGELO

1. St. Peter's Square
2. St. Peter's in the Vatican
3. Historical Artistic Museum
   Treasury of St. Peter's
4. Vatican Palaces
5. Vatican Museums
6. Sistine Chapel
7. Vatican Gardens

The broad Via della Conciliazione leads directly to Vatican City State, the smallest State in the world, which came into being on 11 February 1929 with the signing of the Lateran Pacts. It occupies one three-thousandth of the surface area of the comune of Rome and includes, apart from Vatican City itself, the basilicas of San Giovanni in Laterano, Santa Maria Maggiore and San Paolo fuori le Mura, the Pontifical Palaces of Castelgandolfo, and other areas inside and outside Rome that enjoy the privilege of extraterritoriality.

The symbol and historical centre of the Vatican is the basilica of **St. Peter's** which dominates the vast **square** of the same name, Bernini's masterpiece which was created between 1656 and 1667. The elliptical piazza is 140 m wide and ringed by 284 columns, positioned four deep and topped with statues of saints. At the centre is the Egyptian obelisk that once stood in Nero's Circus. Made of red granite and 25.37 m high, it is the only monolith in Rome to have remained intact. It was inaugurated in its new position on 26 September 1586, and the emblems of Sixtus V were put in place to recall the pope who achieved the enterprise. The cross at the top stands over a reliquary containing a fragment of the True Cross. At either side of the obelisk stand two fine fountains, the one on the right by Maderno, that on the left by Carlo Fontana. Two circular discs set into the paving of the square between the obelisk and the fountains mark the spot from where the viewer gains the impression that Bernini's colonnade is composed of a single row of columns.

As for the St. Peter's Basilica itself, apart from being the very symbol of Christianity, it could also be said to be the emblem of Rome. It's architectural history incorporates three levels: the current building rests on the foundations of Constantine's basilica, which stood for more than a thousand years and in its turn was built over a pagan-Christian burial site.

Constantine began to construct his basilica between 319 and 322 AD, over the site where St. Peter's tomb was venerated, following his martyrdom under Nero between 64 and 67 AD. The facade of the current basilica is accentuated by a great stairway, and the inscription on the frieze bears the name of Pope Paul V who entrusted the work to Maderno. Between the protruding columns are windows, of which the one in the middle is the Loggia of the Blessings, from which the pope imparts his urbi et orbi blessing.

The majestic dome, designed by Michelangelo, has a diameter of 42.5 m and is the largest in the world after that of the Pantheon. The construction history of the entire basilica was long and complicated. At the beginning of the sixteenth century Julius II ordered the old basilica be demolished and entrusted Bramante with the task of building the new one. Over the course of nearly fifty years Bramante's place was taken first by Raphael then by Antonio da Sangallo the Younger. In 1546 the commission passed to Michelangelo who, by rounding-out the four apses and increasing the rake and height of the dome, resting it entirely on four piers, completely revolutionised the design.

After 1564 it fell to Giacomo Della Porta to actually build the immense cupola and finally, in 1607, Paul V (Camillo Borghese) ordered Carlo Maderno to extend the basilica, adding three spans to one of the arms of the Greek cross.

11

12

13

15

14

Access to the building is by five bronze doors located under the broad and decorated atrium (one interesting detail is the seventeenth-century re-working of Giotto's mosaic of the *Navicella*, above the main entrance). The central door is by Filarete (1445) and comes from the old basilica; the one on the left is the Door of Death by Giacomo Manzù (1964), while on the far right is the Holy Door which is only opened during Jubilee Years. Entering the building one is immediately struck by its vast dimensions: it is in fact 186 m long and has a nave and two aisles with side chapels, while the centre of the dome stands at a height of 132.5 m. Having admired the splendid *holy water stoups* supported by cherubs, we move to the first chapel on the right where, behind a thick sheet of glass, is the wonderfully-tender *Pietà* by Michelangelo, a universally-admired work of incomparable beauty from 1499. Next along are the Cappella di San Sebastiano, the Cappella del Santissimo Sacramento with its *tabernacle* by Bernini, and the Cappella Gregoriana. Before reaching the right arm of the transept with the altar to Sts. Processus and Martinian, we come to the venerated bronze statue of *St. Peter*, attributed to Arnolfo di Cambio (thirteenth century). Directly above the tomb of St. Peter is one of the most original architectural works of the Baroque, Bernini's bronze *baldachin* (1633). It has spiral columns decorated with vine stems and swarms of bees recalling the coat-of-arms of Pope Urban VIII to whom the baldachin is dedicated. In front of the altar, steps lead down to the area of the *Confessio*, the work of Maderno, which contains the tomb of St. Peter.

In the apse is the monument of the *Cathedra of St. Peter* (1656), to

16

17

18

19

20

21

22

the right of which is the funerary monument of *Urban VIII* (1647), both masterpieces by Gian Lorenzo Bernini. The funerary monument to the left of the Cathedra is dedicated to *Paul III* and is a sixteenth-century work by Guglielmo Della Porta.

At either side of the apse, in the passages leading, respectively, to the right and left arms of the transept, are funerary monuments to *Clement XIII*, a magnificent piece by Antonio Canova, and to *Alexander VII*, by Gian Lorenzo Bernini.

After the left arm of the transept, passing through the door under the funerary monument of *Pius VIII* by Pietro Tenerani, we come to the sacristy and the famous **Historical Artistic Museum - Treasury of St. Peter's**. Among the many important works it contains we may mention: the *Dalmatic of Charlemagne*, a liturgical vestment once thought to have been donated to Leo III by Charlemagne after his coronation in St. Peter's Basilica in the year 800, but in reality a Byzantine piece of outstanding workmanship from the fifteenth century; the *Sarcophagus of Junius Bassus*, a fourth-century Roman work carved on three sides with scenes from the Old and New Testaments; the funerary monument to *Sixtus IV*, a work in bronze by Antonio del Pollaiolo, and many magnificent examples of the art of liturgical goldsmiths and jewellers over the centuries.

Returning to the church we may admire the Cappella Clementina, the Cappella del Coro and the Cappella della Presentazione, as well as the Cappella del Battesimo with its baptismal font by Carlo Fontana. In the aisle between the latter two chapels, let us not overlook the *Stuart Family Monument*, a work by Antonio Canova from 1817.

One visit not to be missed is the climb up Michelangelo's dome, which can be accomplished entirely on foot or partly by elevator, and which affords the visitor one of the most magnificent and panoramic views of the Eternal City.

The Vatican Grottoes, created in the space between the floor of the old Constantinian basilica and the floor of the current basilica, contain, apart from chapels dedicated to various saints, the tombs of kings, queens and popes from the tenth century on. The grottoes also house the tombs of Paul VI (Giovanni Battista Montini) (1978) and of John Paul II (Karol Wojtyla) (2005).

The most sacred spot is the tomb of St. Peter, under the aedicule built in the fourth century by the emperor Constantine over what was presumed to be the grave of the Apostle of Christ. In one of the chapels around the apse is a fresco attributed to the school of the fourteenth-century Roman painter Pietro Cavallini, the *Madonna della Bocciata*. It is so-called because, according to tradition, during the Sack of Rome in 1527 a drunken soldier, infuriated at having lost a game of bowls (*bocce* in Italian), flung one against the sacred image, striking the face which began to drip blood.

The Vatican necropolis (visits must be booked in advance and access is from the Piazza dei Protomartiri Cristiani to the left of the basilica) is the cemetery in which the grave of the Apostle Peter was located; it was entirely buried when Constantine built the original basilica. Rediscovered in 1941 after excavations ordered by Pope Pius XII, the necropolis still has its original street with mausoleums to either side and the *Campus Petri*, the site in which St. Peter was laid to rest following his martyrdom under Nero.

St. Peter's in the Vatican, Gian Lorenzo Bernini, funerary monument of *Urban VIII*
St. Peter's in the Vatican, Gian Lorenzo Bernini, funerary monument of *Alexander VII*
Historical Artistic Museum - Treasury of St. Peter's, *Sarcophagus of Junius Bassus*
Vatican Grottoes, tomb of *John Paul II*
Historical Artistic Museum - Treasury of St. Peter's, *Antonio del Pollaiolo*, funerary monument of *Sixtus IV*
St. Peter's in the Vatican, *Antonio Canova*, *Stuart Family Monument*

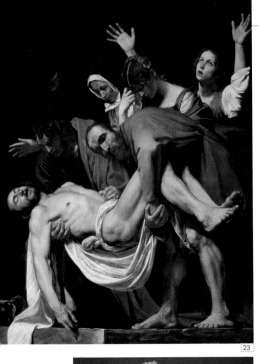

24

25

23

26

28

The **Vatican Palaces**, are a complex of buildings defended by the Swiss Guard, a corps founded in 1506 when Pope Julius II enlisted 200 Swiss soldiers to protect the papal residence. Though their numbers have gradually dropped, the guards continue to serve, wearing their characteristic uniforms designed, it is said, by Michelangelo.

To reach the **Vatican Museums** we must follow Via di Porta Angelica as far as Piazza del Risorgimento, then Via Leone IV and Viale Vaticano until reaching the new entrance, inaugurated for the Jubilee Year 2000.

The Vatican Pinacoteca, housed since 1932 in a building constructed by Luca Beltrami by order of Pius XI, has eighteen rooms divided as follows: Room I, works by the "Primitives", artists active from the twelfth to the fifteenth centuries; Room II, Giotto and his followers; Room III, Fra Angelico, Gentile da Fabriano, Gozzoli and Lippi; Room IV, Melozzo da Forlì and Marco Palmezzano; Room V, minor artists of the 1400s; Room VI, Carlo Crivelli and Niccolò di Liberatore called l'Alunno (fifteenth century); Room VII, Umbrian painters of the 1400s including Perugino and Pinturicchio; Room VIII, Raphael; Room IX, Leonardo da Vinci and various sixteenth-century artists; Room X, Venetian artists of the 1500s including Titian and Veronese; Room XI, sixteenth- and seventeenth-century artists including Barocci, Cavalier d'Arpino and Ludovico Carracci; Room XII, seventeenth-century artists including Domenichino and Caravaggio; Room XIII, seventeenth- and eighteenth-century artists including Nicolas Poussin and Pietro da Cortona; Room XIV, more seventeenth- and eighteenth-century artists including Baciccia, Sassoferrato and Daniel Seghers; Room XV, dedicated to the 1700s with works by Thomas Lawrence, Carlo Maratta and Giuseppe Maria Crespi; Room XVI, works by Wenzel Peter; Room XVII preparatory models for certain works by Gian Lorenzo Bernini in the Vatican Basilica; Room XVIII, collection of icons.

Another Vatican gallery is the Collection of Modern Religious Art which contains religiously-thened pieces by twentieth-century artists. It includes works by De Pisis, De Chirico, Carrà, Manzù, Van Gogh, Paul Gauguin and others.

For sculptures, visit the Pio-Clementino Museum with its sarcophagi, statues and Greek-Roman mosaics. The most famous work is the *Laocoönte*, a magnificently compelling Greek marble group from the first century BC, discovered by chance on 14 January 1506 near the *Domus Aurea*. It is the work of the Rhodian sculptors Agesander, Athenodorus and Polydorus.

27

The *Head of Athena*, discovered near Castel Sant'Angelo, was probably part of the decorations of Hadrian's mausoleum. Only the face is original, the neck and helmet were added to give a sense of completeness to the bust. The *Belvedere Torso* portrays a powerful human torso; other works of notable artistic merit include *Hermes*, the *Apollo Belvedere* and others. The Chiaramonti Museum is equally rich and well-stocked with sarcophagi, bas-reliefs and statues.

Our visit continues with the Museum of the Vatican Apostolic Library. Here is the magnificent Sistine Hall, the great reading room built by Domenico Fontana and named after Pope Sixtus V who ordered the construction; the Gallery of Urban VIII, containing various scientific instruments; the Museo Sacro, with objects discovered in the catacombs; the Room of the Aldobrandini Marriage with its fresco of the Augustan age discovered on the Esquiline Hill at the beginning of the 1600s, and the Chapel of St. Pius V.

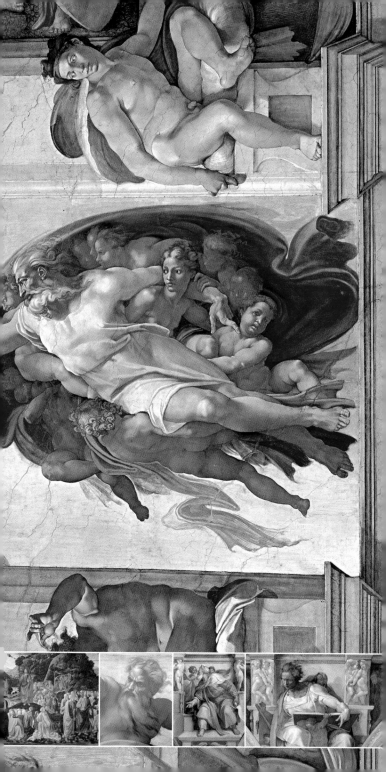

29   30

31

32

The Borgia Apartment, its decorations ordered by Pope Alexander VI who dwelt there, comprises a number of rooms identified by the subjects of their frescos, the work of Pinturicchio and other artists: the Room of the Sibyls, of the Creed, of the Liberal Arts, of the Saints, of the Mysteries, of the Popes, and of the Vestments.

The **Sistine Chapel**, which takes its name from Sixtus IV, is one of the most important and remarkable works of art in the world, universally known for Michelangelo's famous frescos which he painted by commission from several popes: Julius II, Clement VII and Paul III. The chapel - 40.23 m long, 20.7 m high and 13.41 m wide - was built by Giovannino de' Dolci between 1477 and 1480 to a design by Baccio Pontelli.

The side walls are decorated with twelve frescos, with six scenes from the life of Moses and six from the life of Christ by Umbran-Tuscan artists of the 1400s such as Perugino, Botticelli and Ghirlandaio. On the end wall is the majestic *Last Judgement*, a single scene by Michelangelo that revolves around the figure of Christ the Judge. The elect, around and above Christ, arise at the sound of the trumpets, while the damned cannot rise and are dragged down to hell by Minos and Charon.

In the lunettes at the top is the triumph of the symbols of the Passion, with the Column of Flagellation, the Cross and the Crown of Thorns being borne by angels. The Virgin Mary's serene gaze is directed upon the elect. The figures are in large part naked, and deliberately dilated in an allusion to mankind's rebirth free from all the limitations and burdens imposed by nature.

An absolutely enthralling series of figures and biblical scenes extends across the beautiful ceiling.

The famous *ignudi* of the ceiling are simply individual figures of young men, almost a technical experiment in natural poses. The central panels depict, with a quite exceptional dynamism, scenes from Genesis, such as the *Creation of the Sun, Moon and Stars* and the *Separation of Land from Water* where God the Father, suspended over the sea, looks down and makes different gestures with each hand.

The most important fresco, however, is the *Creation of Adam* in which God's finger infuses a soul into man, who is already animate but powerless. Unlike the other animals that walk on all fours, man is shown in the act of raising himself to the upright position.

Finally, in the seven *Prophets* and the five *Sibyls*, all seated on marble thrones adorned with reliefs and pairs of cherubs and angels, Michelangelo creates a variety of poses, characters and ages that transcend the physiognomy of the figures themselves.

Our next stop is the *Stanze* of Raphael which were originally built during the pontificate of Nicholas V. In 1508, Julius II entrusted Raphael with the decoration of the rooms, a task that occupied the artist until his death (1520). There are four frescoed rooms: the Stanza dell'Incendio; the Stanza della Segnatura with its famous *School of Athens*, a true artistic masterpiece; the Stanza d'Eliodoro with the equally famous *Liberation of St. Peter*, and the Sala di Costantino with works by Raphael's pupils.

The Loggia of Raphael is a beautiful gallery of decorated arches, its architecture partly the work of Bramante. The paintings, by Raphael and his school, depict scenes from the Old Testament.

The loggia gives access to the Chapel of Nicholas V, decorated with

SISTINE CHAPEL
CHAPEL OF
NICHOLAS V, FRA
ANGELICO, ST.
PETER CONFERS
THE DIACONATE
UPON ST. STEPHEN,
ST. STEPHEN
DISTRIBUTES ALMS
TO THE POOR
STANZE OF
RAPHAEL,
RAPHAEL, SCHOOL
OF ATHENS
STANZE OF
RAPHAEL,
RAPHAEL,
PARNASUS, DETAIL

33

34

35

frescos by Fra Angelico showing scenes from the *Lives of St. Lawrence and St. Stephen*. From there we pass on to the Gallery of Maps, decorated with maps of Italy, then the Gallery of Tapestries, the Gallery of the Candelabra and the Chariot Room, so called because it houses a fine marble chariot from the first century BC.

Be sure to visit the Etruscan Museum, with its twenty-two rooms containing important collections of terracotta, urns from various periods (note the *Mars of Todi* from the late fifth century BC) and various objects from Etruscan necropolises in central Italy.

The ten rooms of the Egyptian Museum contain sarcophagi, statues, sculptures, statuettes and various other extremely rare artefacts of Egyptian civilisation.

Finally, leaving the museums, we may visit the **Vatican Gardens** which still preserve the structures and characteristics typical of sixteenth-century Italian gardens.

The closest and most breathtaking views of the dome of St. Peter's may be enjoyed from these gardens: an Eden of exotic plants, fountains and architectural gems, artistic treasures that have risen on the hillside which, from the 1500s to today, has surrounded the Apostolic Palaces.

The walls around the gardens of Vatican City State enclose a silent and complex world (there is even a small railway station and a heliport), a silence broken only by the sound of running water and the chirping of the birds.

The enchantment has its culminating point in the Casina di Pio IV, a true pearl of Italian mannerism, built among the loggias and nymphaeums which have become its natural setting.

3 EGYPTIAN
   MUSEUM, ROOM III
4 ETRUSCAN
   MUSEUM,
   ROOM IV
5 PALAZZO DEL
   GOVERNATORATO
6 AERIAL VIEW OF THE
   VATICAN GARDENS
7 CASINA DI PIO IV

Plan of
Vatican City

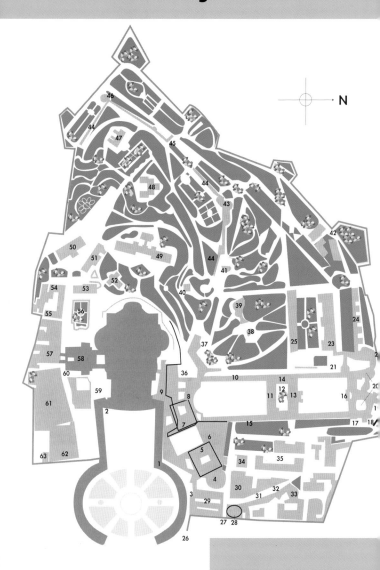

Plan of
St. Peter's Basilica

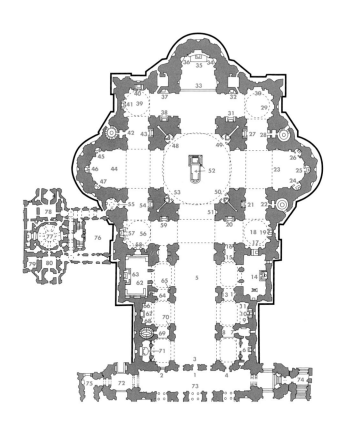

1 Atrium
2 Door of he Dead, by Manzù
3 Central Door, by Filarete
4 Holy Door
5 Central nave
6 Chapel of the Pietà
7 Monument to Leo XII
8 Monument to Queen Christine of Sweden
9 Monument to Pius XI
10 Chapel of St. Sebastian
11 Monument to Pius XII
12 Monument to Innocent XII
13 Monument to Matilde di Canossa
14 Chapel of the Blessed Sacrament
15 Monument to Gregory XIII
16 Monument to Gregory XIV
17 Monument to Gregory XVI
18 Gregorian Chapel
19 Altar of the Madonna del Soccorso
20 Altar of St. Jerome
21 Altar of St. Basil
22 Monument to Benedict XIV
23 Right transept
24 Altar of St. Wenceslas
25 Altar of Sts. Processus and Martinian
26 Altar of St. Erasmus
27 Altar of the Navicella
28 Monument to Clement XIII
29 Altar of St. Michael the Archangel
30 Altar of St. Petronilla
31 Altar of St. Peter restoring Tabitha to life
32 Monument to Clement X
33 Aisle of the Cathedra
34 Monument to Urban VIII
35 Monument to the Cathedra of St. Peter
36 Monument to Paul III
37 Monument to Alexander VIII
38 Altar of St. Peter healing the lame man
39 Chapel of the Madonna della Colonna
40 Altar of St. Leo the Great
41 Altar of the Madonna della Colonna
42 Monument to Alexander VII
43 Altar of the Sacred Heart
44 Left transept
45 Altar of St. Thomas
46 Altar of St. Joseph
47 Altar of the Crucifixion of St. Peter
48 Statue of St. Veronica
49 Statue of St. Helena
50 Statue of St. Longinus
51 Statue of St. Peter
52 Confession and papal altar
53 Statue of St. Andrew
54 Altar of the Bugia
55 Monument to Pius VIII and entrance to the Sacristy and the Treasury
56 Clementine Chapel
57 Altar of St. Gregory
58 Monument to Pius VII
59 Altar of the Transfiguration
60 Monument to Leo XI
61 Monument to Innocent XI
62 Chapel of the Choir
63 Altar to the blessed Virgin immaculate
64 Monument to St. Pius X
65 Monument to Innocent VIII
66 Monument to John XXIII
67 Chapel of the Presentation of the Virgin Maria
68 Monument to Benedict XV
69 Monumento to M. Clementina Sobieski
70 Monument to the last alla Stuarts
71 Baptistery
72 Arch of the Bells
73 Mosaic of the Navicella
74 Equestrian statue of Constantine
75 Equestrian statue of Charlemagne
76 Largo Braschi
77 Sacristy
78 Historical Artistic Musum Treasury of St. Peter's
79 Chapter
80 Sacristy of the Canons

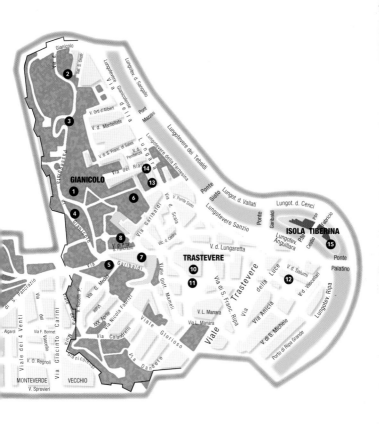

7

8

11

10

T he green hill of the **Janiculum** stretching along the right bank of the Tiber is full of magnificent treasures and wonderful sights to be discovered. On its slopes, in the piazza of the same name, is the church of **Sant'Onofrio** (1439) containing frescos by Baldassarre Peruzzi; adjoining is the convent where the Italian poet Torquato Tasso died in 1595. Continuing up the Passeggiata del Gianicolo, on the left is **Tasso's Oak** where the poet used to sit and meditate and, a little further on, the **Beacon of the Janiculum**, a work by Manfredo Manfredi from 1911, donated by Italians in Argentina.

Having reached **Piazzale Garibaldi** with its monument to the Hero of the Two Worlds by Emilio Gallori (1895), we may pause to enjoy a breathtaking panorama of Rome. Here, at exactly midday every day since 1904, three soldiers load and fire a blank shot from a cannon. The tradition of the cannon shot dates back to Pius IX who, to avoid confusion in times, established the service in 1846. Before coming to the Janiculum, the cannon was fired from the towers of Castel Sant'Angelo and later from Monte Mario.

At the top of the hill, beyond Porta San Pancrazio, is **Villa Doria-Pamphilj**, a large area of greenery created in the seventeenth century by order of Camillo Pamphilj, nephew of Pope Innocent X. It is a vast area of fields, woods, lakes and fountains, filled with beautiful well-proportioned buildings such as the Casino del Bel Respiro, the Casino Corsini, the Doria-Pamphilj funeral chapel, the Giardino del Teatro, the Casino di Allegrezza, the Villa Vecchia, and the Fountains of the Snails, of the Lilies, of Cupid and of Venus.

Descending in the other direction along Via Garibaldi we come to the great Fontana dell'Acqua Paola, built by Paul V in 1612. Nearby is the ninth-century church of San Pietro in Montorio, adjoining which Bramante's stupendous **Tempietto** stands on the site where St. Peter is said to have been crucified.

Further down Via Garibaldi is one of the most arcane, fascinating and least-known places in the city, the **Bosco Parrasio** or Teatro degli Arcadi, an architectural gem designed by Francesco De Sanctis who also built the Spanish Steps. It is structured as a three-level garden, at the top of which is a small palazzo with a concave facade, the work of Francesco Azzurri.

At the bottom of Via Garibaldi we come to the Porta Settimiana, to the left of which, in the grounds of Palazzo Corsini, are the **Botanical Gardens**. With a surface area of 12,000 m², around 2,000 m² of greenhouses and 3,500 plant species, it is one of the largest in Italy and certainly one of the most active in terms of the transmission of knowledge on plants and the environment. The plant collections are particularly interesting, not just for their scientific importance but, especially, for the method of cultivation and the reconstruction of environments, which helps visitors in the difficult task of imagining the species in their areas of origin.

In the lee of the Janiculum the city's most typical and popular district, **Trastevere**, lies in an area that used to be occupied by the Etruscans. Much later its streets and alleys came to be inhabited by craftsmen, grooms and cooks whose job it was to serve the notables of the time; thus grew a fiercely proud neighbourhood with lay and libertarian tendencies, well expressed in the monument to the Roman dialect poet *Gioacchino Belli* which stands in the piazza of the same name. Apart from the famous old *osterie* (true citadels of traditional Roman cuisine), the many sites to visit include: the church of San Giovanni Battista dei

PASSEGGIATA DEL GIANICOLO
BEACON OF THE JANICULUM
AERIAL VIEW OF SANTA MARIA IN TRASTEVERE
SANTA CECILIA, NAVE
BOTANICCAL GARDENS, FONTANA DEI TRITONI
ISOLA TIBERINA
FONTANA DELL'ACQUA PAOLA (VIA GARIBALDI)
EMILIO GALLORI, MONUMENT TO GIUSEPPE GARIBALDI
TASSO'S OAK
BRAMANTE'S TEMPIETTO
VILLA DORIA-PAMPHILJ, CASINO DEL BEL RESPSIRO
SANTA MARIA IN TRASTEVERE

13

14

15

16

Genovesi with attached cloister of the 1400s, the hospice of San Michele, and the basilicas of **Santa Maria in Trastevere** and **Santa Cecilia**. The former, founded by St. Calixtus in the third century, has a portico added by Carlo Fontana in the eighteenth century. It stands in one of Rome's most characteristic squares, one of the oldest in the city, decorated with a fountain which is also the work of Carlo Fontana. The interior, with a nave and two aisles, has a wooden ceiling by Domenichino from 1617, while the presbytery contains the *Fons Olei*, the place where in 38 BC oil mysteriously gushed forth pre-announcing the coming of the Saviour. The basilica of Santa Cecilia was built in the fifth century over a pre-existing Roman building. Access is now by a monumental entrance attributed to Ferdinando Fuga (eighteenth century). The interior, with a nave and two aisles, contains the ancient *caldarium* where St. Cecilia is said to have been tortured, the *ciborium* by Arnolfo di Cambio (1283) and a statue of the saint by Stefano Maderno.

Finally, we must nor forget to admire two buildings facing one another in Via della Lungara: Palazzo Corsini and Villa Farnesina. **Palazzo Corsini** was built by Ferdinando Fuga in 1732, over the earlier Palazzo Riario. It is the headquarters of the Accademia Nazionale dei Lincei, and houses a section of the Galleria Nazionale d'Arte Antica - the main part of which is in Palazzo Barberini - with works by Van Dyck, Rubens and Caravaggio and his followers. **Villa Farnesina** is a Renaissance work by Baldassarre Peruzzi (1508) built for the famous banker Agostino Chigi who used it to entertain princes and popes. The inner loggia was frescoed by Raphael's pupils to drawings by their master; note the *Story of Psyche*. The loggia leads to the Sala di Galatea with the fresco of that name, a famous piece by Raphael himself. On the first floor, in Agostino Chigi's bedroom, are Sodoma's splendid frescoes from 1517; particularly outstanding is the *Marriage of Alexander and Roxana*.

Having walked down the Lungotevere degli Anguillara we find ourselves facing the **Isola Tiberina**, linked to the mainland by two historic bridges: Ponte Cestio, built by Lucius Cestius in 46 BC and rebuilt at the end of the 1800s, and Ponte Fabricio on the left bank of the river, also known as Quattro Capi because of the pair of four-faced Roman hermae on the parapet. It was built by Lucius Fabricius in 62 BC and has been restored a number of times over the centuries after floods of the Tiber. In the Middle Ages it was known as Ponte dei Giudei because it linked the island to the Jewish Ghetto. Further south is the Ponte Rotto, the only surviving arch of the Ponte Emilio, the first stone bridge, built between 179 and 142 BC. Despite the fact that it has been a ruin since the sixteenth century, it still conserves all its ancient fascination.

The Isola Tiberina is of probable volcanic origin, and rose over the centuries with the accumulation of alluvial deposits. Having the form of a ship, in antiquity the Temple of Jupiter was built on the "bow" and the Temple of Aesculapius on the "stern", while an obelisk represented the mainmast "amidships" on the spot where a spire built by Ignazio Jacometti in 1869 now stands in front of the ancient church of San Bartolomeo, which dates from the tenth century but was much restored in 1624. In the Middle Ages, a convent of Benedictine sisters was built on the island, its place taken around the mid 1500s by a hospital run by the religious order of Fatebenefratelli, who used the old building as a place to care for the sick. Also present on the island is the confraternity of the Sacconi Rossi, whose mission it is to gather and bury the corpses of the drowned.

Itinerary no. 8

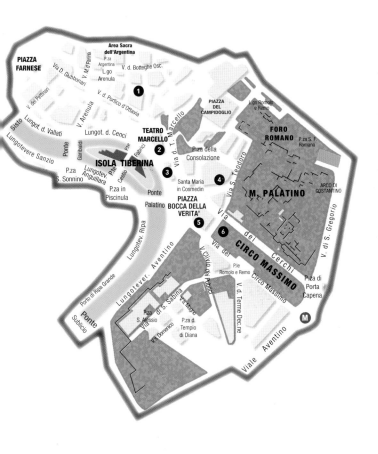

❶ Fontana delle Tartarughe

❷ Theatre of Marcellus

❸ Forum Boarium

❹ San Giorgio in Velabro

❺ Santa Maria in Cosmedin

❻ Circus Maximus

12

At the end of Via dei Funari is Piazza Mattei where we may admire the splendid and unusual **Fontana delle Tartarughe**, a work by Taddeo Landini and Giacomo Della Porta (1584), one of the most exquisite and elegant masterpieces in Europe in its conception and realisation, especially in the figures of the youths delicately pushing the tortoises up to drink from the basin above.

The **Theatre of Marcellus**, the only ancient theatre to survive in Rome, was erected by Augustus in 13 BC in honour of his prematurely-deceased nephew Marcellus.

The extremely imposing edifice, which was originally constituted of three levels of barrel-vaulted arches, served as a model for building the Colosseum. The importance of this theatre is also due to the fact that it was conceived in a manner entirely different from Greek theatres.

Piazza della Bocca della Verità marks the location of the ancient **Forum Boarium**, which includes the eleventh-century Casa dei Crescenzi, a fortress with Roman remains and decorations; the Temple of Fortuna Virilis, now identified as the Temple of Portunus, from the second or first century BC; and the circular Temple of Vesta with its Corinthian colonnade. Facing these is the Arch of Janus (from *ianus*, a passageway) dating from the age of Constantine (fourth century) and, behind that, the sixth-century church of **San Giorgio in Velabro** with its original portico and a twelfth-century campanile. Resting against the church is the third-century AD Arch of the Money-Changers, dedicated to Septimius Severus and Julia Domna.

The church takes its name from *Velabrum*, the swamp where Faustulus found Romulus and Remus.

Facing the church is the fascinating Cloaca Maxima, a masterpiece of Roman engineering that gathered water from the surrounding heights and channelled it into the Tiber.

The nearby church of **Santa Maria in Cosmedin**, from the sixth century with subsequent transformations, has a fine twelfth-century campanile and an interesting arched portico with pilasters (the only mediaeval example of its kind in Rome), preceded by a *protiro*.

Under the portico, on the left, is the *Bocca della Verità*, a drain cover from the classical period depicting the mask of a river god which, according to legend, has the power to bite off the hand of anyone who tells lies. Facing the church is the Fontana dei Tritoni by Francesco Carlo Bizzaccheri from 1715.

Beyond is Piazzale Ugo La Malfa with its monument to *Giuseppe Mazzini*, a work by Ettore Ferrari from 1929. It overlooks the **Circus Maximus**, 600 m long and said to have been constructed at the time of Tarquinius Priscus, though later transformed and embellished by Caesar, by Augustus (who built the imperial box and raised the obelisk now in Piazza del Popolo), and by Constantine's son Costantius II (who ordered the erection of a second obelisk, now in Piazza San Giovanni in Laterano). The circus could accommodate up to 300,000 spectators and remained in use until 549.

1. Porta San Paolo
2. Pyramid of Caius Cestius
3. San Paolo fuori le Mura
4. Baths of Caracalla
5. Arch of Drusus
6. Porta San Sebastiano

   Museo delle Mura

The Lungotevere Aventino and Via Marmorata (to the right of which, our backs to the river, is Monte Testaccio) bring us to **Porta San Paolo** and the **Pyramid of Caius Cestius**. The pyramid marks the perimeter of the Protestant cemetery where non-Catholics were laid to rest, alongside actors and prostitutes to whom the Church forbade a consecrated burial. Porta San Paolo corresponds to the ancient Porta Ostiense, a gate in the Aurelian Walls ordered by Aurelian himself in the third century, and restructured in the fifth by Honorius, who closed one of the original openings. To the left is the pyramid (12 BC), 27 m high and conserving the remains of the tribune Caius Cestius.

Following Via Ostiense we come to the basilica of **San Paolo fuori le Mura**, the largest after St. Peter's, built by Constantine in 324 over the tomb of the Apostle Paul but, unfortunately, completely destroyed by fire in 1823. Guglielmo Calderini's quadriporticus (1892), with 146 columns and the statue of *St. Paul* at the centre, precedes the facade with its fine mosaic to a design by Filippo Agricola. The grandiose interior is 131 m long and 65 m wide, and has a nave and four aisles separated by 80 monolithic columns. It faithfully reproduces (though without quite recreating the original atmosphere) the dimensions of the ancient basilica, of which all that remains is the eleventh-century bronze Byzantine door, to the right of the central portal as one looks at the facade; the fifth-century mosaics of the triumphal arch, and the beautiful thirteenth-century tabernacle by Arnolfo di Cambio. The coffered ceiling is very fine, and the mosaic medallions under the side windows with portraits of all the popes from St. Peter to the present are also interesting. Particularly worthy of attention is the stupendous cloister, untouched by the fire, one of the finest works by the Vassalletto family (1214) with its paired straight and spiral colonnettes over which runs a mosaic entablature.

Continuing along Via Ostiense then turning into Via Laurentina, we

12

13

14

come to the Abbazia delle Tre Fontane, built on the site where St. Paul is traditionally held to have been beheaded.

Returning to Porta San Paolo and following the entire length of Viale Aventino, off to our right are the magnificent remains of the **Baths of Caracalla**, breathtakingly-grandiose in their immensity. Built by Caracalla between 212 and 217 AD, the complex originally measured 337 m by 328 m and could contain around 1600 bathers. Before reaching the central pool (*natatio*), customers would go to the changing area (*apodyterium*) from where the circuit would begin with sporting activities, either outside or indoors. The *laconicum* (Turkish bath), a rectangular room with small oblique openings to prevent the dispersion of the heat, gave access to the *calidarium*, a great circular hall 34 m in diameter with a large round basin of hot water in the middle. The circuit thus-far described could also be followed from the other side of the building, perfectly identical to this. From here the route was just one and continued with the *tepidarium*, a small warm room, then the *frigidarium*, a central hall in the form of a basilica, to conclude in the *natatio* or open-air swimming pool. Over the course of the centuries, extraordinary works of art have been found in the baths, such as the two giant Farnese sculptures discovered in the 1500s: the *Bull* and *Hercules*, now kept in the Museo Archeologico Nazionale in Naples; the mosaic with *Athletes*, discovered in 1824 and now in the Vatican Museums, and the two granite basins which form the fountains in Piazza Farnese.

Via di Porta San Sebastiano is a picturesque and isolated road running between high walls and archaeological remains. On the right is the church of San Cesareo, rebuilt in the sixteenth century and notable for its Cosmati work. Nearby is the house of Cardinal Bessarion (at no. 8), a delightful fifteenth-century construction with Renaissance furniture and an ornamental garden. The tomb of the Scipios (at no. 9), from the Republican age, conserves the remains of various sarcophagi of that noble Roman family. In the adjoining park is the Columbarium of Pomponius Hylas with first-century urns and paintings. The **Arch of Drusus** at the end of Via di Porta San Sebastiano dates from the third century and once supported the Antonine aqueduct which brought water to the Baths of Caracalla. Having thus reached **Porta San Sebastiano**, the largest and best-preserved of the gates in the Aurelian Walls, we can visit the interesting **Museo delle Mura** which documents this history of the walls of Rome from their construction to the twentieth century.

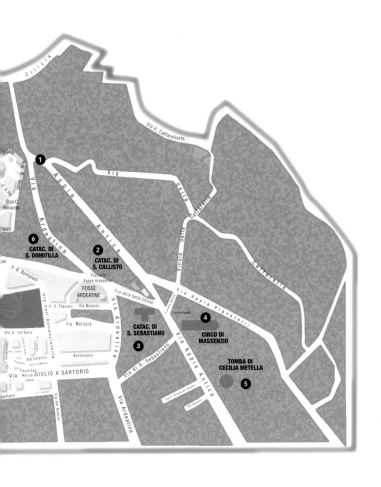

1. Via Appia Antica
2. Catacombs of San Callisto
3. Catacombs of San Sebastiano
4. Circus of Maxentius
5. Tomb of Cecilia Metella
6. Catacombs of Domitilla

5

6

7

8

9

10

The **Via Appia Antica**, *Regina Viarum*, the most important of the Roman roads, was built by Appius Claudius in 312 BC to link Rome and Capua, then extended in 190 BC to reach Brindisi. Many are the funerary monuments, the villas and the catacombs along this picturesque stretch of ancient highway which we will now consider in some detail. The church of *Domine quo vadis?*, rebuilt in the 1600s, stands on the spot where tradition holds that Peter, fleeing Rome, met Jesus and asked him: "Lord, where are you going?". Jesus replied: "I am going to be crucified again!" at which it is said that Peter turned and went back to face martyrdom. The interior contains a cast of the footprints which, the legend says, Christ left in the road surface. The original stone is kept in the basilica of San Sebastiano. Near the Via Ardeatina are the Fosse Ardeatine, where the German occupying troops massacred 335 Italians on 24 March 1944.

The **Catacombs of San Callisto**, which date from the third century, are some of the best preserved of their kind. The name comes from Pope Calixtus, and they were used to bury a number of martyred pontiffs such as Pontian, Fabian and Sixtus II. The body of St Cecilia, martyred under the emperor Marcus Aurelius, was also discovered intact here. One element of great artistic value is the Cubiculum of the Sacraments with third-century paintings symbolising Baptism and the Eucharist.

The **Catacombs of San Sebastiano** stretch for some 12 km. They originally arose from a pozzuolana quarry that was used first as a pagan burial site (second century AD), then as a Christian cemetery named after Sts. Peter and Paul who were believed to have been buried there. The word catacomb used to designate the quarry in question clearly derives from the Greek *katà kymbas*, which means 'near the cavity'. The catacombs, then, are cemeteries; not places where the Christians lived but where they buried their dead and prayed, immersed in spirituality far from the bustle of daily life. It must also not be forgotten that by Roman law the dead had to be buried outside the city walls, both for hygienic and moral reasons. The current basilica was dedicated to St. Sebastian in the sixth century to honour this martyred, an officer of the Praetorian guard who was pierced with arrows and beaten with iron bars in the year 298. Inside the building it is possible to visit the crypt and the tomb of St. Sebastian, near to which is a fine bust of the saint which has been attributed to Bernini. The current church covers only the area of the nave of the original *Basilica Apostolorum*. In the catacombs thenselves, arranged over three levels where the temperature remains constant, we may see three different kinds of burial site: the horizontal loculus in which the body was placed wrapped in a shroud; the arcosolium, a grave surmounted by an arch in sign of glory to indicate the last resting place of a martyr, and the sarcophagus, a stone coffin decorated with bas-reliefs as an indication of nobility and wealth. The area was oxygenated with black maidenhair ferns which hung from large openings in the roof. In the past, many of the loculi were broken open by Barbarians in search of gold or Christians seeking relics. If many of the bricks have the imperial seal, this is due to the fact that terracotta was a State monopoly. The many small loculi were used for the bodies of children, and give us some idea how high infant mortality was at that time. The various forms of graffiti are easily-interpretable Christian symbols: fish = Christ; palm = martyr; anchor = hope; dove = soul.

11

12

To reach the place where the remains of Sts. Peter and Paul were placed in 258 AD, we must climb a stairway leading to a third-century oratory. Here the wall plaster is scored with around 500 pieces of graffiti written by pilgrims leaving praises, prayers and supplications to the two Apostles, whose bodies lay here for at least 55 years. About 300 metres beyond San Sebastiano, to the left, is the **Circus of Maxentius**, built by that emperor in 309 AD. It was linked by a gallery to the adjoining imperial palace. Facing it is the mausoleum of Romulus, Maxentius' son who died in infancy.

The **Tomb of Cecilia Metella** is the most famous monument on the Via Appia and has an inscription to its occupant, the wife of Crassus. It is a large cylindrical tower some 20 metres in diameter, dressed in travertine and topped with high Ghibelline battlements which were added in 1302. Next to the tomb stand the remains of the mediaeval castle of the Caetani family (fourteenth century). Opposite are the ruins of the Gothic church of San Nicola, with an interesting campanile.

The **Catacombs of Domitilla** on the Via Ardeatina take their name from an imperial family all of whose members suffered martyrdom in the second century AD. A fourth-century basilica with a nave and side aisles stands over the grave of the martyrs Nereus and Achilleus; it contains interesting allegorical frescoes depicting *St. Petronilla*, the *Miracle of the Fountain*, the *Saviour among the Apostles*, and the famous *Scene of the Epiphany*.

Away to the left of the Via Appia we can see the Alban Hills, on the slopes of which are the Castelli Romani , typical and picturesque villages set amid the rolling hilly landscape.

If we continue further along the Via Appia, we may admire further remains of Roman tombs in an inspirational setting, redolent of myth and legend.

MAUSOLEUM OF ROMULUS

TOMB OF CECILIA METELLA

CATACOMBS OF DOMITILLA, ARCOSOLIUM OF VENERANDA

CATACOMBS OF DOMITILLA, *SAVIOUR AMONG THE APOSTLES*

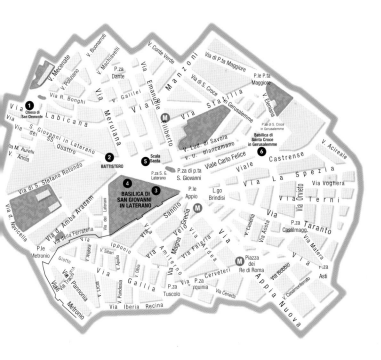

1 Basilica of San Clemente

2 Baptistery of San Giovanni in Laterano

3 Basilica of San Giovanni in Laterano

4 Palazzo Lateranense

5 Scala Santa

6 Basilica of Santa Croce
in Gerusalemme

This itinerary starts at the beginning of Via San Giovanni in Laterano, near the basilica of **San Clemente** which takes its name from Clement, fourth pope of the Church of Rome. The upper church, built in the twelfth century, was modernised in the eighteenth century. The interior - reached by passing under a *protiro* and crossing a mediaeval quadriporticus - still contains frescoes by Masolino da Panicale with *Scenes from the Life of St. Catherine of Alexandria* (1431), and a splendid twelfth-century mosaic depicting the *Triumph of the Cross* in the apse.

From the church we descend into the mysterious and fascinating crypt, where remains of other sacred buildings that occupied this site over the centuries are still to be seen. The first part is Romanesque, then we come to the basilica with a nave, side aisles and a mediaeval apse before, finally, reaching the Roman section. Various artefacts unearthed beneath the paleo-Christian basilica are to be seen on the walls. The Triclinium was used for the worship of the god Mithras, a cult which first arose in Iran, spread as far as Italy, then dissolved in the fourth-century partly as a result of having been banned by imperial edict.

Continuing to the end of Via San Giovanni in Laterano we come to the piazza of the same name, dominated by the obelisk of Sixtus V (the oldest and tallest of the surviving obelisks in Rome) which is 32.18 m high, not counting the base. Made of red granite and covered with hieroglyphics indicating the date of the reign of Tuthmosis III (1504-1450 BC), Constantine ordered it be transported to Alexandria; however he died while it was en route and his son Constantius II had the monolith brought to Rome, on an enormous vessel especially built for the purpose. In 357 AD the obelisk was erected in the Circus Maximus where it remained until 10 August 1588, when it was definitively transferred to its current location. On the right of the square stands the **Baptistery of San Giovanni in Laterano**, ordered by Constantine and rebuilt by Sixtus III in the fifth century. The octagonal interior has double columns with an architrave supporting the dome. Of the four chapels, the fourth, dedicated to St. John the Evangelist, still has bronze doors from 1196 and, on the ceiling, sixth-century mosaics with symbolic animals.

11

The great basilica of **San Giovanni in Laterano** dates from the fourth century but has been enlarged and transformed on a number of occasions by such famous architects as Domenico Fontana and Francesco Borromini. The facade, by Alessandro Galilei, has a majestic giant order of columns, with 15 statues over the architrave.

The interior, accessed by one of five doors, is in the form of a Latin cross and has a nave with four side aisles, some 130 m long. Apart from the beautiful Cosmatesque floor from the time of Martin V (1417-1431) and the superlative wooden Renaissance ceiling, it also has a magnificent transept decorated for the Jubilee 1600 and a pointed baldachin from 1357, under which is the papal altar. From the transept we may visit the Treasury Museum and, from the last chapel on the left, the beautiful cloister by the Vassalletto family (1215-1230) with its twin colonnettes and mosaic frieze.

Next to the basilica is the magnificent and austere **Palazzo Lateranense**, papal residence from the time of Constantine until 1377, when the Holy See was moved to the Vatican. Next to the piazza is the palazzo containing the **Scala Santa**, built by Domenico Fontana for Sixtus V in 1590. Tradition identifies this stairway as the one Jesus climbed to appear before Pontius Pilate. There are 28 wood-covered steps which the faithful ascend on their knees in prayer. They lead to the Chapel of St. Lawrence or *Sancta Sanctorum*, decorated with thirteenth-century Cosmatesque mosaics and containing many sacred relics.

Ultimately we take Viale Carlo Felice, running along the Aurelian Walls, to reach the basilica of **Santa Croce in Gerusalemme**. Standing in the piazza of the same name, it was built by Constantine in 320 to house the relics of the True Cross brought from Palestine by his mother St. Helena. The church has been much restored and reconstructed, especially in the 1600s and 1700s, as evinced by the Baroque facade and the Romanesque campanile. Inside we may admire the fine apse fresco of the *Triumph of the Cross*, perhaps the work of Antoniazzo Romano (1492), and the tomb of *Cardinale Francesco Quiñones* by Jacopo Sansovino (1536). From the right aisle it is possible to descend to the Chapel of St. Helena with its splendid fifth-century ceiling mosaic, restored by Melozzo da Forlì in the late 1400s. At the end of the left aisle is the entrance to the Chapel of the Relics, containing holy relics of the True Cross.

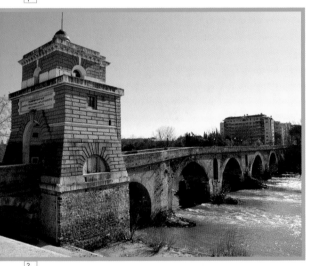

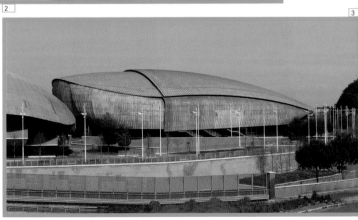

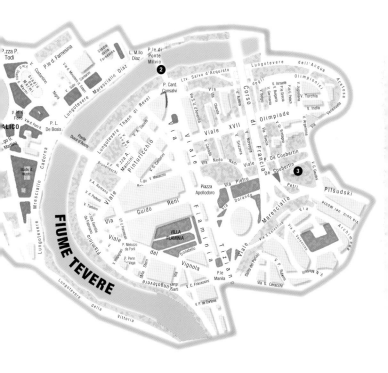

 Foro Italico

 Ponte Milvio

 Auditorium 'Parco della Musica'

4

5

H aving walked the considerable length of Viale Angelico, we come to the **Foro Italico**, a sports complex overlooking the Lungotevere with many buildings and installations, among them the Stadio Olimpico, the Stadio del Nuoto, the Stadio dei Marmi, the Stadio del Tennis and the headquarters of the Italian National Olympic Committee.

Here between 1928 and 1932 the architect Enrico Del Debbio, taking ancient Greece as his model, created what was originally called the Foro Mussolini, ordered by the fascist regime to exalt the physical strength and beauty of Italian youth. One of the more important works is the Stadio dei Marmi, from 1932, with its 60 statues of naked young athletes wrestling, running, or throwing the discus or the javelin, almost a continuation of the art of Michelangelo.

Along Viale del Foro Italico (formerly Viale dell'Impero) are mosaics executed to drawings by Gino Severini, Angelo Canevari, Achille Capizzano and Giulio Rosso. The Viale ends in the piazza of the same name, at the centre of which is the Fontana della Sfera, a work by Mario Paniconi and Giulio Pediconi.

Not far from the Foro Italico is the Milivan Bridge, **Ponte Milvio**, also called *Ponte Mollo*, built by the censor Marco Aemilius Scaurus in 109 BC to replace a wooden bridge that had been in service since the third century BC.

In Viale Pietro de Coubertin on the left bank of the Tiber, the side opposite the Foro Italico, is the **Auditorium 'Parco della Musica'**, designed by the architect Renzo Piano and built between 1995 and the early years of the twenty-first century. The structure is made up of three great concert halls of differing sizes, lined with wooden panelling and arranged around a *cavea*, an open-air amphitheatre with space for around 3,000 spectators. The complex also includes a restaurant, a bookshop and two permanent exhibitions: an archaeological museum with exhibits found during the course of building work, and the Museo degli Strumenti Musicali dell'Accademia Nazionale di Santa Cecilia, one of the most important collections of its kind in Italy, the central nucleus of which is made up of instruments from the Italian lute-making tradition from the seventeenth to the twentieth centuries.

STADIO DEI MARMI
PONTE MILVIO
AUDITORIUM
'PARCO DELLA
MUSICA'
STADIO OLIMPICO
PONTE MILVIO,
DETAIL
AUDITORIUM
'PARCO DELLA
MUSICA'

6

Museums of Rome

ARCHAEOLOGICAL MUSEUMS

Antiquarium Forense
piazza Santa Maria Nova, 53 - tel. 06 6990110

Museo delle Antichità Etrusco Italiche
piazzale Aldo Moro, 5 - tel. 06 49913315
www.uniroma1.it/musei/indexmusei2.asp

Museo dell'Ara Pacis
lungotevere in Augusta - 06 82059127
www.arapacis.it

Museo dell'Arte Classica - Gipsoteca
piazzale Aldo Moro, 5 - tel. 06 49913960
www.uniroma1.it/musei/indexmusei2.asp

Museo Barracco
corso Vittorio Emanuele II, 166/a - tel. 06 68214105
www.museobarracco.it

Musei Capitolini
piazza del Campidoglio, 1 - tel. 06 82059127
www.museicapitolini.org

Museo della Civiltà Romana, Planetario e Museo Astronomico
piazza Giovanni Agnelli, 10 - tel. 06 5422919
www.museociviltaromana.it
www.planetarioroma.it

Museo delle Mura
via di Porta San Sebastiano, 18 - tel. 06 70475284
www.museodellemuraroma.it/

Museo Nazionale d'Arte Orientale
via Merulana, 248 - tel. 06 4874415
www.museorientale.it/

Museo Nazionale Etrusco di Villa Giulia
piazzale di Villa Giulia, 9 - tel. 06 3200562
www.villaborghese.it

Museo Nazionale Preistorico Etnografico 'Luigi Pigorini'
piazzale Guglielmo Marconi, 14 - tel. 06 549521
www.pigorini.arti.beniculturali.it

Museo Nazionale Romano
Palazzo Massimo
largo di Villa Peretti, 1 - tel. 06 4814144
for bookings: 06 39967700
www.archeorm.arti.beniculturali.it
Terme di Diocleziano
via Enrico De Nicola, 78 - tel. 06 47826152

MUSEO BARRACCO, GREEK-ROMAN SECTION

MUSEO CAPITOLINO, SALA DEL GLADIATORE

MUSEO NAZIONALE PREISTORICO ETNOGRAFICO 'LUIGI PIGORINI', MOSAIC MASK

EQUESTRIAN STATUE OF MARCUS AURELIUS

5

6

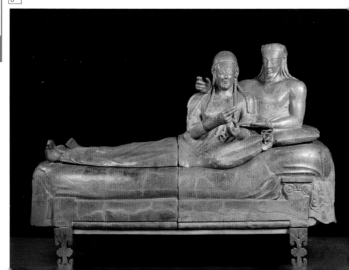

for bookings: 06 39967700
www.archeorm.arti.beniculturali.it

Aula Ottagona o della Minerva
via Romita, 8 - tel. 06 4880530
for bookings: 06 39967700
www.archeorm.arti.beniculturali.it

Palazzo Altemps
piazza Sant'Apollinare, 44 - tel. 06 6833759
for bookings: 06 39967700
www.archeorm.arti.beniculturali.it

Crypta Balbi
via delle Botteghe Oscure, 31 - tel. 06 39967700
for bookings: 06 39967700
www.archeorm.arti.beniculturali.it

Museo della via Ostiense
via Raffaele Persichetti, 3 - tel. 06 5743193

MEDIAEVAL AND MODERN MUSEMS

Casino dell'Aurora Pallavicini
via XXIV Maggio, 43 - tel. 06 4742615
www.casinoaurorapallavicini.it/

Galleria dell'Accademia Nazionale di San Luca
piazza dell'Accademia di San Luca, 77
tel. 06 6798850 / 06 6790324
www.accademiasanluca.it

Galleria Borghese
piazzale del Museo Borghese - tel. 06 32651329
www.galleriaborghese.it/borghese/it

Galleria Colonna
via della Pilotta, 17 - tel. 06 6784350
www.galleriacolonna.it

Galleria Comunale d'Arte Moderna e Contemporanea
via Francesco Crispi, 24 - tel. 06 4742848
www2.comune.roma.it/avi/

Galleria Doria-Pamphilj
piazza del Collegio Romano, 2 - tel. 06 6797323
www.doriapamphilj.it

Galleria Nazionale d'Arte Antica di Palazzo Barberini
via Barberini, 18 - tel. 06 4824184
www.galleriaborghese.it/barberini/it

Galleria Nazionale d'Arte Moderna
viale delle Belle Arti, 131
tel. 06 322981
www.gnam.arti.beniculturali.it

10

11

12

14

15

13

16

Galleria Nazionale di Palazzo Corsini
via della Lungara, 10 - tel. 06 68802323
www.galleriaborghese.it/corsini/it

Galleria Spada
piazza Capodiferro, 13 - tel. 06 6832409
www.galleriaborghese.it/spada/it

Museo dell'Alto Medioevo
viale Abramo Lincoln, 3 - tel. 06 54228199

Museo Pietro Canonica a Villa Borghese
viale Pietro Canonica, 2 - tel. 06 82059127
www.museocanonica.it

Museo Napoleonico
piazza di Ponte Umberto I, 1- tel. 06 68806286
www.museonapoleonico.it

Museo Nazionale di Castel Sant'Angelo
lungotevere Castello, 50 - tel. 06 6819111
www.castelsantangelo.com

Museo Nazionale di Palazzo Venezia
via del Plebiscito, 118 - tel. 06 699941
www.galleriaborghese.it/nuove/spvenezia.htm

Museo di Roma
piazza San Pantaleo, 10 - tel. 06 67108346
www.museodiroma.it

Museo di Roma in Trastevere
piazza Sant'Egidio, 1/b - tel. 06 5816563
www.museodiromaintrastevere.it

Museo della Zecca
Palazzo dei Ministeri Finanziari
via XX settembre, 97 - tel. 06 47613317 www.museozecca.ipzs.it/

MILITARY MUSEUMS

Museo dell'Istituto Storico e di Cultura dell'Arma del Genio
Lungotevere della Vittoria, 31 - tel. 06 3725446
www.esercito.difesa.it/root/musei/museo_genio.asp

Museo Sacrario delle Bandiere delle Forze Armate
Vittoriano, via dei Fori Imperiali
piazza Venezia - tel. 06 47355002
www.museimilitari.it

Museo Storico dell'Arma dei Carabinieri
piazza Risorgimento, 46 - tel. 06 6896696
www.carabinieri.it/Internet/Arma/Ieri/MuseoStorico/

GALLERIA COLONNA, GREAT HALL

GALLERIA COLONNA, BRONZINO, *VENUS, CUPID AND A SATYR, DETAIL*

GALLERIA COLONNA, ANNIBALE CARRACCI, *PEASANT EATING BEANS*

GALLERIA NAZIONALE D'ARTE MODERNA, VINCENT VAN GOGH, *L'ARLESIENNE (PORTRAIT OF MADAME GINOUX)*

GALLERIA NAZIONALE D'ARTE MODERNA, INTERIOR

GALLERIA NAZIONALE D'ARTE MODERNA, INTERIOR

GALLERIA DELL'ACCADEMIA DI SAN LUCA, GIUSEPPE GRASSI, *PORTRAIT OF VINCENZO CAMUCCINI*

17

18

19

2

Museo Storico dei Bersaglieri
piazzale di Porta Pia - tel. 06 486723
www.museimilitari.it

Museo Storico della Fanteria
piazza Santa Croce in Gerusalemme, 9 - tel. 06 7027971
www.museimilitari.it

Museo Storico dei Granatieri di Sardegna
piazza Santa Croce in Gerusalemme, 7 - tel. 06 7028287
www.museimilitari.it

Museo Storico della Guardia di Finanza
piazza Mariano Armellini, 20
tel. 06 44238841
www.museimilitari.it

Museo Storico della Liberazione di Roma
via Tasso, 145 - tel. 06 7003866
www.istituticulturali.it/moduli/istcult/istituto.jsp?idIstituto=315

Museo Storico della Motorizzazione Militare
Cecchignola, viale dell'Esercito, 170 - tel. 06 5011885
www.museimilitari.it

23

24

25

26

RELIGIOUS MUSEUMS

Museo delle Catacombe di San Sebastiano
via Appia Antica, 136 - tel. 06 7850350
www.catacombe.org/

Museo Ebraico di Roma
Sinagoga, lungotevere de' Cenci, 15
tel: 06 68400661
www.museoebraico.roma.it/

Museo del Monastero di San Paolo
Basilica di San Paolo
piazzale San Paolo - tel. 06 5410341
www.abbaziasanpaolo.net

Museo di San Giovanni in Laterano
Basilica di San Giovanni in Laterano
piazza di Porta San Giovanni - tel. 06 69886433

Museo di San Pancrazio
Basilica di San Pancrazio
piazza di San Pancrazio, 5/d - tel. 06 5810458

Museo del Presepio Tipologico Internazionale
via Tor de' Conti, 31/a - tel. 06 6796146

MUSEUMS OF VATICAN CITY

Museo Filatelico e Numismatico
viale Vaticano - tel. 06 69883005
www.vaticanstate.va/IT/News/nuovo_museo_filatelico_e_numismatico.htm

Museo Storico Artistico - Tesoro di San Pietro
piazza San Pietro (ingresso all'interno della Basilica Vaticana) - tel. 06 39967450

Museo Storico Vaticano e Appartamento papale
piazza San Giovanni in Laterano
tel. 06 69886386

Musei Vaticani
viale Vaticano, 100 - tel. 06 69883860 / 06 69884341
http://mv.vatican.va

Roman cookery

fresh tomato bruschetta

SERVES 4/6

- 4 ripe tomatoes, seeded and diced
- 2 tablespoons red onion, diced
- 2 tablespoons extra-virgin olive oil, plus extra
- ½ garlic clove
- 4 leaves fresh basil, torn into small pieces
- salt and freshly ground pepper
- 4 slices crusty Italian bread

PREPARATION: In a small bowl, mix tomatoes with minced onion, 2 tablespoons of olive oil and the basil, and season with salt and pepper • Lightly toast the bread on a grill or under the broiler, and rub with the cut side of the garlic • Arrange the garlic toast on a platter, sprinkle with salt and drizzle generously with olive oil • Spoon the tomato mixture on top of each piece of toast, and serve immediately

Mozzarella in carrozza

SERVES 4

- flour for dredging
- salt and freshly ground pepper
- 8 slices white bread, crusts removed, cut in ½ diagonal
- 4 thick slices fresh mozzarella, cut in ½ diagonally
- 2 anchovy fillets, chopped
- ½ cup cold whole milk
- olive oil for frying
- 2 eggs

PREPARATION: Place the flour in a bowl, and season it with salt and pepper • Lay ½ of the slices of the bread on a flat work surface • Top each with a slice of mozzarella and ½ anchovy • Top with a piece of bread, and dip each sandwich in the milk • Dredge each sandwich in the seasoned flour, shaking off the excess • In a large skillet with high sides, warm 1 inch of olive oil until shimmering • In a bowl, beat the eggs, and season with salt and pepper • Dip each sandwich into the beaten egg mixture • Carefully place each sandwich into the skillet with the hot oil, and fry until golden on each side • Remove from skillet, drain on paper towels and sprinkle with additional salt before serving.

Stuffed rice balls

MAKES 16

- 1¾ cup boiled rice cooked al dente (or leftover risotto)

FOR THE RAGÙ AND FILLING
- 1 tablespoon extra-virgin olive oil
- 1 small onion, diced
- 1 carrot, peeled and diced
- 1 stalk celery, diced
- ½ pound ground lamb
- ½ cup red wine
- 1 cup canned whole, peeled tomatoes, drained and chopped
- 4 ounces fresh mozzarella, cut into 16 small cubes
- 3 eggs, beaten
- salt and freshly ground pepper
- 1 cup bread crumbs
- olive oil for frying

PREPARATION FOR THE RICE BALLS: With wet hands, form 16 balls of seasoned rise or leftover risotto • Poke a hole in each ball with your thumb, and make a little space inside • Fill each one with a chunk of mozzarella • Seal the opening with another dollop of seasoned rise or leftover risotto • Roll each ball in beaten egg, then bread crumbs seasoned with salt and pepper • Warm olive oil over medium-high heat in a heavy-bottomed pot • Deep-fry in batches until golden-brown • Drain on paper towels • Serve immediately.

PREPARATION FOR THE RAGÙ: In a skillet, heat extra-virgin olive oil • Add onion, celery, carrot and lamb; stir until meat is cooked through and onion is translucent • Deglaze with wine • Add tomatoes; cook until ragù reaches a dense texture • Add salt to taste • Season the boiled rise with ragù and let it cool down.

Penne all'arrabbiata

SERVES 4

- 2 tablespoons extra-virgin olive oil
- 2 cloves garlic, crushed
- ½ teaspoon crushed red pepper flakes
- 18 ounces peeled tomatoes, seeds removed
- salt
- 1 tablespoon chopped parsley
- 14 ounces penne pasta

PREPARATION: Bring a large pot of water to a boil. • In a large skillet over medium-high heat, warm the oil • Add the pepper flakes and the garlic cloves, and sauté until they soften and turn golden • Remove and discard the garlic and pepper flakes, and add the tomatoes • Season with salt and cook for 15 minutes • While the sauce is cooking, salt the water and add the pasta • Cook the pasta until al dente, drain, and transfer the pasta to the skillet with the sauce and toss it over medium-high heat • Transfer the pasta into a heated serving dish and sprinkle it with the chopped parsley.

Bucatini alla amatriciana

SERVES 4

- 5 ounces guanciale (available at gourmet stores) or bacon, chopped
- 3 ripe tomatoes, peeled, seeded and chopped
- ½ teaspoon crushed red pepper flakes
- salt and freshly ground pepper
- 14 ounces bucatini pasta
- ⅓ cup pecorino romano, grated
- extra-virgin olive oil

PREPARATION: Bring a large pot of water to a boil • In a saucepan over medium-high heat, add the extra-virgin olive oil and the guanciale and cook until the meat slightly crisps, 6 to 8 minutes • Remove the guanciale and set aside • Add the tomatoes to the pan, then add the crushed red pepper flakes and season with salt and pepper • Cook for 10 minutes, then return the guanciale pieces to the sauce to reheat. • While the sauce is cooking, salt the water and add the pasta • Cook the bucatini until al dente, drain and toss with the sauce • Top with the pecorino and serve warm.

Linguine with clams

SERVES 4

- 1½ pounds littleneck clams, soaked in cold water for 30 minutes, drained
- salt
- 1 pound linguine
- 2 tablespoons extra-virgin olive oil
- 1 clove garlic, peeled
- ½ cup white wine
- freshly ground pepper
- 1 tablespoon chopped parsley

PREPARATION: Place the clams in a pot with 1 cup of water • Cover, and place over medium heat for 4 minutes, or until they open • Drain, reserving the cooking liquid • Bring a large pot of water to a boil. • Add salt and the pasta, and cook until al dente • In a skillet over medium heat, warm the olive oil • Add the garlic, and sauté for 1 minute • Discard the garlic clove, and add the wine and reserved cooking liquid. • Season with salt and pepper, and simmer until reduced slightly • Drain the pasta, and add it to the skillet along with the clams • Garnish with the parsley, and serve.

Pasta e ceci

SERVES 4

- 8 ounces dried chickpeas, soaked in water overnight and drained
- 1 sprig of rosemary or (as an alternative) 2 bay leaves
- 1 pound lagane or pappardelle pasta
- 3 tablespoons extra-virgin olive oil
- 1 clove garlic
- 2 ounces sun-dried or peeled tomatoes, roughly chopped
- salt and freshly ground pepper

PREPARATION: Place the chickpeas in a pot. Cover with water, and add salt • Simmer over medium-low heat for about 3 hours • When half cooking time is passed, remove 2 spoonfuls of chickpeas and purée until smooth • Return the chickpeas mixture into the pot and continue to cook for the remaining time • In a deep skillet over medium heat, warm 3 tablespoons of olive oil, add the rosemary, the garlic and the chopped tomatoes and cook for 10 minutes • Turn off the heat, remove the garlic and pour this sauce into the pot with the chickpeas, stir and add salt, if necessary • Add the pasta and cook until al dente • Place the soup in a serving bowl and season with olive oil and pepper.

Saltimbocca alla romana

SERVES 8

- 3 ounces prosciutto, thinly sliced
- 8 sage leaves
- 8 slices of veal, 6 to 8 ounces each
- ¼ cup flour
- 4 tablespoons butter
- ¾ cup dry white wine
- salt and freshly ground pepper

PREPARATION: Place half a slice of prosciutto on each slice of veal and top with a sage leaf • Cover with plastic wrap • On a clean work surface, pound the veal slices with a meat mallet to ¼-inch thick, until the prosciutto and sage are embedded in the veal • Dust both sides with flour • In a large skillet over medium-high heat, warm the butter and arrange the veal slices in the pan • Sauté the veal until golden brown on both sides. • Remove the veal from the skillet and place in a serving platter • Add the wine to the skillet and scrape up any browned bits from the bottom of the pan • Simmer over medium-high heat until it thickens slightly. • Pour the sauce over the saltimbocca, and serve.

Abbacchio alla cacciatora

SERVES **4/6**

- 2 cloves garlic, crushed
- 1 teaspoon rosemary, chopped
- 2 anchovies, roughly chopped
- 1 cup white wine vinegar
- 2 pounds leg of spring lamb (suckling lamb), cut into ¾-inch pieces
- salt and freshly ground pepper
- ¼ cup extra-virgin olive oil
- 1 cup dry white wine

PREPARATION: Using a mortar and pestle or a blender, crush garlic, rosemary and anchovies into a paste • Add the vinegar a little at a time, stirring until the sauce is well blended • Transfer to a bowl and cover • In a skillet over medium-high heat, warm the olive oil and add the lamb pieces seasoned with salt and pepper • Sauté until well browned on all sides • Pour in the wine and bring to a simmer, then add the vinegar sauce • Reduce the heat, cover and cook for 2 hours, stirring often • Allow to sit for at least 30 minutes before serving.

INDEX OF PLACES

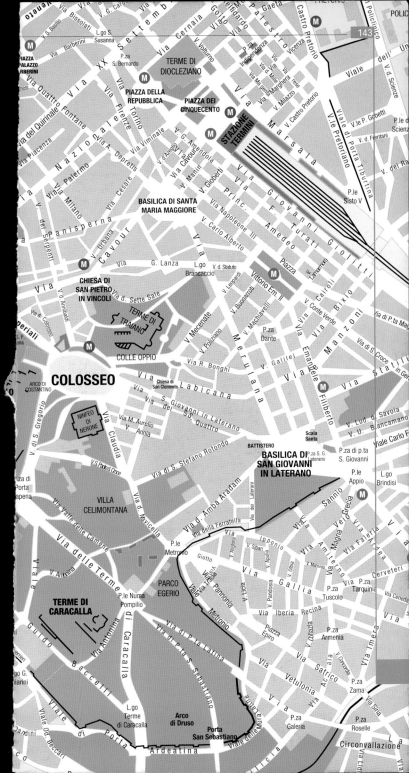

© Copyright 2009
This book has been edited and published by
ATS Italia Editrice s.r.l.
via di Brava, 41/43 - 00163 Roma
tel. +39 0666415961 - fax +39 0666512461 - www.atsitalia.it
No part of this book may be reproduced

Editorial co-ordination *Frida Giannini*
Editor *Paola Ciogli*
Photo research *Angela Giommi*
Graphic design, layout and cover *Sabrina Moroni*
Scanning and colour correction *Leandro Ricci*
Technical co-ordination *Flavio Zancla*
Translation *Piers Amodia*
Printing *Kina Italia-L.E.G.O.*
Photographs *Photographic archive Ats Italia Editrice*
Photographic archive Vatican Museums
Photographic archive Fabbrica di San Pietro
Photographic archive Electa

*The publisher may be notified concerning
any unidentified iconographic sources*

Questo volume è disponibile anche in lingua italiana
Ce volume est disponible aussi en français
Dieser Band ist auch in deutscher Sprache erhältlich
Esta obra también está publicada en español
Настоящая книга вышла также на русском языке

ISBN 978-88-7571-771-1